THE ENFIELD POLTERGEIST TAPES

One of the most disturbing cases in history.
What really happened?

BY

DR MELVYN J. WILLIN

www.whitecrowbooks.com

The Enfield Poltergeist Tapes

Published in the United States of America and the United Kingdom by White Crow Books; an imprint of White Crow Productions Ltd.

For information, contact White Crow Books
@ info@whitecrowbooks.com.

Cover Design by Astrid@Astridpaints.com
Interior design by Velin@Perseus-Design.com

Paperback ISBN: 978-1-78677-073-8
eBook   ISBN: 978-1-78677-074-5

Non-Fiction / Body, Mind & Spirit / Parapsychology / Death & Dying

www.whitecrowbooks.com

PRAISE FOR
THE ENFIELD
POLTERGEIST TAPES

The Enfield Poltergeist became and has remained one of the best-known cases of its kind, not least perhaps because its somewhat dramatic nature and its human interest have sustained several television programmes and assorted publications. It has, however, been eyed in less friendly fashion by various of the more austere members of the psychical research community and certain other persons of a sceptical disposition. The result has been a good deal of sometimes acrimonious dispute. In this situation Dr.Willin's new volume is particularly welcome. It contains a considerable amount of hitherto unpublished information – indeed quite possibly more first-hand information about the case than has ever appeared before in one volume. And its approach to the numerous clashes of opinion is commendably balanced. It is one of the rare books to which one can truthfully apply the hackneyed claim that within its designated area it is essential reading.

The Enfield Poltergeist Case, a much-publicised set of events, needs occasional fresh scrutiny and analysis. This study by Dr Willin fulfils this need admirably; there is a fresh and close examination of the audio records, and interviews with witnesses, which re-evaluate and enrich the amount of available data. This is a painstaking investigation that will become an essential part of the literature.

~ **PROFESSOR JOHN POYNTON**, VICE-PRESIDENT, SOCIETY FOR PSYCHICAL RESEARCH.

Dr Willin has performed a valuable service in transcribing and presenting Maurice Grosse's Enfield poltergeist tapes so that readers can judge for themselves how far the material supports the positive views expressed by Guy Lyon Playfair in *This house is haunted*.

~ **MARY ROSE BARRINGTON**, CHAIRMAN OF THE ENFIELD POLTERGEIST INVESTIGATION COMMITTEE, AUTHOR OF *TALKING ABOUT PSYCHICAL RESEARCH: THOUGHTS ON LIFE, DEATH AND THE NATURE OF REALITY.*

The Enfield poltergeist is one of the most famous psychical research investigations of the twentieth century. But between the sensationalised accounts in the media and the more sceptical (unpublished) report of the Society for Psychical Research, where lies the truth? As the archive liaison officer for the Society, custodian of the tape recordings from the case, and a friend of the primary investigators, Dr Willin is in a unique position to present the evidence, so that readers can decide for themselves. We may never know for sure but the result is an engrossing perspective on this unique case.

~ **PROFESSOR BERNARD CARR**, PROFESSOR OF MATHEMATICS AND ASTRONOMY AT QUEEN MARY UNIVERSITY OF LONDON.

ALSO BY THE AUTHOR

Music, Witchcraft and the Paranormal.
ISBN 1-905226-18-7

Paranormal Caught on Film.
ISBN-13: 978-0-7153-2980-1

Monsters Caught on Film.
ISBN-13: 978-0-7153-3774-5

Ghosts Caught on Film.
ISBN-13: 978-0-7153-2728-9

CONTENTS

ACKNOWLEDGEMENTS

The production of this book would not have been possible without the co-operation of the Society for Psychical Research, which holds the copyright of the tape recordings that were bequeathed to it after the deaths of Maurice Grosse and Guy Lyon Playfair who made the original recordings. I also acknowledge Jason Engwer's financial generosity during the transcription of the tapes.

When Grosse and Playfair undertook their extensive research for the 'Enfield Poltergeist Case' they received the consent of many people to be recorded during their investigations. There are too many to be named here but I freely acknowledge the part they played in their initial research.

If anyone believes that they should have been acknowledged here then I ask that they contact the publisher to allow further editions of this work to rectify this.

Finally I must acknowledge the support given to me by Jon Beecher at White Crow Books who made this publication possible.

PREFACE

D o not buy this book if you want to read a biased account of the famous 'Enfield Poltergeist Case' from 1977 through to 1978. There are many other choices you could make (see the bibliography) which will either try to convince you of the genuineness of the phenomena produced or its fraudulent origins according to the interpretation of the authors concerned. I do not mind whether you have a wide-open mind or a totally closed one, since I shall not be trying to convince you one way or the other.

Do buy this book if you want to know what really happened!

I have listened and transcribed all of the several hundred audio tapes that were made by Maurice Grosse and Guy Playfair during their investigation of the alleged poltergeist case that took place in Enfield some forty years ago and I shall present, in chronological order, what occurred. It will then be your decision as to whether you believe the phenomena came from spirit entities; psychic forces; mistaken interpretations; hallucinations; naughty children or any other source you might wish to present. I shall strive very hard not to be influenced by what I have read, however intelligent it might be, and instead rely on my ears to describe what was happening according to the audio tapes.

I shall leave out the many hours of general conversation that took place between the parties concerned since I do not believe that the reader will be particularly interested in the weather; special offers in the local supermarket; or what happened in Coronation Street … except, of course, when any of these discussions may have been pertinent to the phenomena. Despite this there will be times when you may wonder why I have included episodes which may be of little interest to the reader. In this respect I agree with Guy Lyon Playfair who wrote:

> … repetitiveness and general confusion are well-established features of poltergeist activity, and I have felt obliged to record the tedious episodes of this very complicated case as well as the exciting ones. (Playfair, 2007, p. x)

He was, perhaps, reiterating the words of the poet Robert Graves who once wrote "[poltergeists] show an appalling sameness of behaviour, humourless, pointless, uncoordinated") (cited Allen, 1994, p. 20).

I shall include some of the more humorous occurrences since the events occasionally demanded this, offering perhaps some light relief from the sometimes all-pervading chaos. Because of their age some of the audio tapes were corrupted beyond recognition and, at other times, the sound quality was poor. I have, therefore, had to listen very carefully to unravel the indistinct voices especially when people were talking at the same time or were not specifically identified by name. There was substantial screaming at times, which made it difficult to distinguish between the children concerned, so I may have attributed the wrong name to a 'screamer' at times... sorry, but I've tried to get it right! The language used is sometimes extremely crude, abusive and sexually explicit, so the reader should be aware that parts of the book should be 'X' rated, as films used to be in bygone days.

I shall also present some details from the extremely well-informed Society for Psychical Research (hereafter SPR) Report that was compiled since it wished to investigate the phenomena and the claims in as much detail as possible. The full report is available in the SPR Library in London.

Although Playfair's book presented the case with considerable reference to Maurice Grosse, he (Grosse) also documented his own personal thoughts about the case in 'The Maurice Grosse Collection' which I catalogued on his behalf and placed in the SPR collection at Cambridge University Library. His comments provide further light on the investigation, which are confirmed by cross-referencing with the tapes, his personal documents and the video diaries he produced.

Almost inevitably the more sensational aspects of the media have equated the Enfield occurrences with the fictional book and subsequent film *The Exorcist*. This story was based on a series of real-life events, which I shall scrutinize to show the obvious parallels and differences between the cases. Once again, ultimately it will be the reader's decision as to where his/her verdict lies.

If all this hasn't put you off then read on and prepare to possibly find out what happened in Enfield from August 31, 1977 onwards.

ABOUT THE AUTHOR

Dr Melvyn Willin has researched alleged paranormal phenomena for over twenty-five years
and has two doctorates in related aspects of
the subject. His own research has included the place of
music in alleged cases of paranormality; the efficacy of
witchcraft spells; and the veracity of claims about supernatural powers within martial arts. He is the honorary archives liaison officer and a council member of
the Society for Psychical Research and a consultant to
the Ghost Club. He has published many articles and
several books on a variety of themes within psychical
research. He has been the custodian of the 'Enfield Poltergeist' tapes since the deaths of Maurice Grosse and
Guy Lyon Playfair and he has transcribed and digitized
the complete collection. He knew both men personally and shared many hours of conversation with them
about the case.

INTRODUCTION

The transcription and digitalization of just over two hundred cassette tapes recorded in the 1970s brought with it a unique set of problems, which needed to be overcome before the task in hand could be attempted. To summarize:

1. Was the tape broken and, if so, repairable?
2. Did the tape play correctly or did the speed change anywhere?
3. Was the content audible throughout?
4. Did the tape begin at the start of Side A or Side B or halfway through, for instance?
5. Were there gaps where the taping process was flawed?
6. Was the label on the cassette holder the same as what was on the tape?
7. What was on the tape? (This involved recognising numerous different people living/ now deceased and understanding the actual content which was not always apparent.)
8. Was the tape able to be digitized if required?

The quality of the tapes used varied, as did their degree of deterioration. Some of them were indeed broken and required specialist repair to make them playable once again and then digitized. This was sometimes not apparent until I was halfway through listening to find a flaw in the cassette or in the actual taping process. Considerable frustration was experienced by trying to transcribe tapes that did not start at the beginning of Side A, but possibly halfway through Side B and then reverted to Side A again. This was exacerbated when previously used tapes presented totally unrelated material in the middle of an investigation or report. Did I mention that what was written on the cassette case did not necessarily relate to what had actually been recorded!

The audibility of the content was undoubtedly the biggest problem. Most of the time Maurice Grosse stood close to the microphone and enunciated clearly. However, other people present were often further away from the microphone and could, therefore, barely be heard. The oft-spoken of 'knockings' were frequently inaudible, which was particularly exasperating when the people present were discussing them at length. Guy Playfair's diction was not as succinct as Grosse's, but he used better quality tapes, which partly compensated for this. As stated previously, the girls Janet and Margaret Hodgson sounded somewhat similar on the tapes, especially when screaming or speaking in the gruff male voices they used, which made their specific identities unclear at times. With everyone talking at once on occasions, trying to work out who was saying what was another problem. Multiple visits by the same people allowed a degree of voice recognition and Grosse was generally good at announcing who was present, but this was not always the case, whereupon a degree of audio-detective work was necessary to figure out who was actually present.

For purposes of clarification I shall not continuously use such words as 'allegedly' or 'purportedly' since it makes the text unduly pedantic. Similarly I shall not continuously use explicit swear words, but having identified what was exactly being said I shall use terms such as "swearing continued" which I am sure the reader will comprehend. When events can be heard on the tapes I shall describe them as such, but only suggest my own interpretation when I feel it is demanded and then I shall identify this as such. Quotation marks will be used when direct speech is used otherwise paraphrasing will be adopted to convey the gist of what was happening or being spoken by the commentators and interviewees. Grosse was particularly keen to record the experiences of the witnesses of the phenomena and frequently narrated events himself. Because some of the tapes were used for multiple recordings, as previously stated, and not always identified as such, some of the dates may not follow strict chronological order in terms of the exact day of the week. However, the months and, of course, the year of the events described will be precise. By combining Playfair and Grosse's tapes, all the recorded material will be presented as succinctly as possible. Some of the dialogue will appear to be both very confusing and contradictory because, in reality, it was indeed so. The names and identities of the 'Voices' coming from the children – and notably Janet – frequently changed. The various voices that the children used will be identified as 'Voice/s' or when the identity is clearly specified such as 'Bill', 'Fred' etc. then that name will be used and the gender referred to accordingly. When seemingly repetitious events occurred they will be indicated, but only when coming from different sources. (Playfair copied some of Grosse's tapes for his own database.) Recordings were not made at the beginning of the case as the investigators did not know what was to follow, which is why the first date recorded was September 1977 (see appendix 3). In addition to the cassettes, two reel-to-reel recordings were discovered in the Maurice Grosse Collection, in December 2018, the contents of which were not identified on the containers. When these were professionally cleaned-up and converted to CDs it was discovered that they only recorded material that had already been digitized by myself from the cassettes.

With the exception of Playfair's book where pseudonyms were mainly used, most of the names of the people involved in the case have been recorded in the public domain and I shall not, therefore, change them. I shall use the names of people as they were known at the time of the investigation and not identify them by their current names – through marriage for instance – unless they happen to be the same. When first names were used I shall follow this procedure, for instance, for the names of the children involved.

The Hodgson family were the main focus of the events that occurred consisting of the divorced mother Mrs Hodgson (47 years), Margaret (13 years), Janet (11 years), Johnny (10 years) and Billy (7 years). The father apparently only visited the house briefly for the purpose of making maintenance payments and Johnny was away at a boarding school for much of the time. The Burcombe family lived a few doors away and John was Mrs Hodgson's brother. Sylvie was his wife and they had two children, Denise and Paul. The Hodgsons' next door neighbours, Vic and Peggy Nottingham, and their son, Gary, also witnessed the occurrences. Other people including the police and members of the public also provided testaments during the course of the investigation.

The main investigators were Maurice Grosse and Guy Lyon Playfair, the latter having had previous experience in exploring alleged poltergeist cases. They were joined at various times by other members of the Society for Psychical Research who prepared a detailed report (see Chapter 2). Psychics, mediums and the press also visited the Hodgson household on various occasions.

CHAPTER ONE

The Grosse/Playfair Tapes

Background

The 'Maurice Grosse Collection' belonging to the SPR and housed at Cambridge University Library contains much of the background information for this case and I quote directly from Playfair's notes therein as follows:

> Mrs Hodgson appears to be a very capable woman who is working under extreme difficulties through lack of money. The house is in a bad state of repair and the furnishings are very poor. The children

however are well cared for and they appear altogether to be a happy unit. Mrs Hodgson has been divorced for about three years. Mr Hodgson is partially spastic with paralysis on his right side. He has been in Claybury Hospital a few times with treatment for a mental (?) condition. Mr Hodgson was mentally disturbed. Margaret appears to be quite a normal child but inclined to be over-emotional. She cries very easily. She goes to special classes as she has been rather backward in her school work. Janet appears to be a reasonably bright child but rather excitable with a strong imagination. She went to a new school at the beginning of September and showed a great deal of apprehension in having to start. She took a couple of weeks to settle down, but, considering all the upsets caused by the disturbances, she's settled in very well. This girl appears to be the epicentre. Johnny was only in the house on one day when I was called in on the case. He goes to a special school – boarding – at Wavendon, Milton Keynes. He is a mentally disturbed child. Billy appears to be a normally intelligent child but he has a bad speech defect. He runs his words together and he is very difficult to understand. He is receiving speech therapy.

The house is a small semi-detached council house built in the late twenties or early thirties. Four different sets of people have lived in the house but there is no available history of the families that have lived there. There do not appear to be any cases of unusual deaths taking place in the house. Some of the furniture and curtains in the house originally came from a house where a small child of four was murdered by her father. Mr Hodgson was friendly with this man and when he eventually committed suicide, Mr Hodgson bought some of the suicide's furniture into his own house.

There is a budgerigar and a goldfish in the house. The budgerigar was given to the family by Mr Richardson and it had belonged to an old lady who had died. The phenomena did start shortly after the bird came into the house.

The relations involved in the case are as follows. Mr John Burcombe, brother to Mrs Hodgson, and deputy head-porter in the hospital: a down-to-earth intelligent man who appears to have a well-ordered mind. Mrs Sylvie Burcombe, his wife, a housewife, with rather a nervous disposition, but alert. Their son, Paul, aged 12 – a lively intelligent boy – and their daughter Denise, 15, (?) also a lively intelligent girl. The neighbours directly involved in this case are the people living in the house next door. Mr Nottingham, about 40, well-built, helpful with a good disposition. Mrs Peggy Nottingham, a key figure in this case, about 38: a strong, rather dominant type, competent and extremely helpful, highly critical and sceptical witness. Their son Gary, late teens: a well-built, healthy-looking individual. Mr Richardson, Mrs Nottingham's father, who was in temporary residence with her: aged 72, physically ailing but mentally alert.

There were no recordings made of the events that occurred at the Hodgson family home on 31 August 1977, so there is no audio evidence as such. According to Playfair's book *This House is Haunted* sounds of knocking were heard and a "heavy chest of drawers" moved of its own accord along the floor. The next-door neighbours, Mr and Mrs Nottingham, were alerted, but could find no natural explanations so they called the police who attended promptly. WPC Heeps and her colleague arrived and Heeps, the Hodgson family and the Nottinghams witnessed a chair sliding across the floor several feet. Over the next few days the family were bombarded with flying marbles and bits of the plastic toy Lego from an unknown source. Mrs Nottingham phoned the *Daily Mirror* to see if they could help and the reporter Douglas Bence and photographer Graham Morris duly turned up on 5 September. Further reporters and photographers followed who were suitably impressed by the genuineness of the family's assertions, especially when they witnessed various phenomena themselves. It was suggested that the SPR should be contacted since the organization had a long history of knowledge in such matters. After receiving a phone call from George Fallows the Society's secretary Eleanor O'Keeffe contacted a new member who had expressed an interest in undertaking investigative work. He was a successful inventor who conveniently lived in London and was able to travel to Enfield without too much difficulty. His name was Maurice Grosse and he had joined the SPR after the tragic death of his daughter in a motorbike accident. After Grosse had experienced what he believed to be poltergeist phenomena himself at the Enfield house, he asked at a monthly SPR meeting, coincidently devoted to poltergeist studies, whether anyone would be interested in helping him with the case and Lawrence Berger (a London dental surgeon) volunteered. A few days later Guy Lyon Playfair (an author and experienced investigator) decided to join Grosse and lend his support. From this time onwards Grosse and Playfair spent many hours at the Hodgson household and recorded hundreds of hours of audio-information taking the form of an actual soundtrack of the phenomena as well as first-hand reports by many of the people who experienced incidents there. The rappings and knocking sounds from Enfield and other similar phenomena were later analysed by Barrie Colvin (2010) and he provided detailed information about the differences between intentionally produced raps and alleged paranormal examples. In the 'Discussion of results' from his report he concluded that there appeared to be "reasonable grounds for concluding that unexplained rapping effects ... exhibit an unusual acoustic waveform pattern" and that the "... generally recognised description of the rap-like sounds often reported at poltergeist investigations [were] not actually raps at all."

What follows is an account of what was actually recorded by Grosse and Playfair between September 1977 and 1997.

September 1977

The first recording was made by Playfair on 19 September "just after 10:00 p.m. when the first bit of Lego had been thrown". There were no recorded sounds other than creaks and miscellaneous noises that were probably caused by normal household activity. Playfair narrated that a chair had turned over but in a different room and was therefore not picked up by the tape recorder. There were only a few more taped sessions up until the end of the month, but one particularly dramatic episode on 21 September concerned the sound of a fairly large chest of drawers turning over seemingly by themselves since no immediate previous sounds were heard: e.g. creaking floorboards as if someone was approaching them and then manually turning them over. Grosse and Playfair both taped the accounts of Mrs Hodgson and John Burcombe of what they claimed to have witnessed including the movement of other furniture and a pillow from the bed.

October 1977

October was a busy month for recording testimonies and phenomena, most of which happened at bedtime for the family after 9:00 p.m. and sometimes stretching well into the night/early morning. The month started with the arrival of the medium Maisie Besant and her directing partner E. Butler who undertook mediumistic sessions. She spoke as if in a trance but failed to provide any verifiable information. During the first half of the month there were numerous witnesses to a wide range of different phenomena. They included Mrs Nottingham who discovered an unexplained pool of water; a bathroom light swinging; the movement of a toilet brush and the toilet flushing of its own accord. Mrs Hodgson, who had been advised by Grosse to keep a diary of incidents, related "noises being heard"; objects falling over; a drawer opening of its own accord and, on several occasions, a bedroom lamp being thrown. Furthermore, she felt as if there was something like a cat pressing down on her legs when in bed. She complained of a headache just before things started to happen, but "not like a normal headache". She suggested that mice might be responsible for some of the activity, but certainly not all of it. Grosse witnessed a slipper flying through the air, which, he believed, was impossible to have been thrown by anyone present and he also heard the collapse of a camp bed, which was in use. He was not in the room at the time but outside. When he and Playfair were worried about their tape-recorders being tampered with, both Janet and Margaret strenuously denied any involvement. Billy was present for many of these incidents and he seemed worried about them. Screams from the girls were frequently emitted immediately after something had been thrown. John Burcombe added his own list of witnessed phenomena including loud "dull thuds" and a light, which seemed to have a mind of its own that actually scared him at the top of the stairs in the house.

On 3 October a meeting was held at Janet's school with the headmaster, members of the local authority, Mrs Hodgson and Grosse, which he taped, with their permission. It was stated that Janet was so tired, at times, that she had to sleep in the school medical room. It was also mentioned that she might be taken into care as a 'holiday' for a week. Janet was showing an abnormal amount of stress at the entry into her new school.

The phenomena continued unabated throughout October. A list of incidents witnessed multiple times by some or all of the family as well as the Nottinghams from next door and members of the Burcombe family included:

- Furniture turning over (chairs, a stool and a heavy sofa and armchair); drawers opening of their own accord and a camp bed collapsing.
- Bedroom objects "flying over" including a lamp and slippers several times.

- Kitchen objects moving (crockery, a teapot and a washing basket) and "cream crackers jumping".
- Bathroom objects moving (a toothbrush, beaker, toilet brush) and unaccounted quantities of water appearing on the floor.
- Unaccounted knockings, rappings, bangings etc.
- The appearances of shadowy figures and "what looked like an old lady at the window".
- A doll's house roof split; a jigsaw puzzle that "shot off the top of a cupboard".
- Crying, whimpering and whispering sounds were also heard.

At various times throughout the investigation Grosse interviewed everyone present, and especially the girls, about the incidents and he was occasionally suspicious about what was going on. Janet could be heard giggling and Grosse would complain about her "sliding out of bed" and with her hand being seen just before a slipper went flying. Both he and Mrs Hodgson became understandably irritated at these times and the girls were threatened with dire consequences if they were "fooling around".

A new direction was instigated by Grosse to try to achieve some sort of communication with whatever was causing the knockings and he tried question and answer sessions via tapping. This produced a communicator referring to itself/herself as "Mrs Haylock". John Burcombe and Grosse attempted to clarify what the actual identity or source of the knocking was, but without much success other than the 'entity' saying it was looking for a glass ashtray that was in the house when it/she lived there. The rappings sometimes transformed into the rhythms of TV themes and such-like and were accompanied by objects (a doll, a box of toys, slippers etc.) being thrown across the room amidst a general commotion. In desperation Grosse attempted gentle hypnosis to try to get Janet, in particular, to go to sleep. This ended October 1977. [The Enfield council arranged for the family to take a week's holiday at Clacton-on-Sea from 29 October to 5 November and details of paranormal activity were not recorded, if they happened, while they were there.]

November 1977

November's taping started on the fifth and, subsequently, there were some occasional background sounds from the celebrations traditionally held on that date. The bangs of fireworks are very different from the rappings that persisted and Grosse continued to attempt communication via the knocks. His patience must have been tested considerably when the raps replied with such rhythms as da-dada-da-da da-da and then the "spirit contact" changed from being "Mrs Haylock" to "Mrs Oakland" and the ashtray sought became wooden when it was previously stated as being made of glass.

Amongst the large number of objects thrown, moved or tipped over, one was of particular importance to Grosse, which is clearly recorded on tape. One must remember that many of the incidents were either recounted to the investigators or occurred in a different room from where they were positioned. However, on 5 November between 10:00 p.m. and 11:00 p.m. Grosse asked whether the spirit was "having a game with him".

Immediately a 'whooshing' sound was heard as a box was hurled across the room at him and hit him on the head. He was suitably shocked and, if one listens to the exclamations from the several witnesses, so was everyone else! The remainder of the evening continued with a picture being pulled off a wall behind where Grosse was positioned; a pillow was thrown; the kitchen table was "thrown over"; the laundry basket was upturned; the kettle "jumped across the kitchen" and bedclothes were repeatedly pulled off the bed.

7 November brought some new events into the chaotic household, namely Janet's being seemingly thrown out of bed with claims of levitation. From the eyewitness descriptions and a dramatic photograph taken by Graham Morris it appeared that she was repeatedly thrown anything from four and a half feet to six feet in the air. Later on in the month Margaret also claimed to be "pulled out of bed". When some of these events happened, Janet looked as if she was asleep and, at times, all three children (the two girls and Billy) were "seemingly dreaming simultaneously".

Mrs Hodgson's "frontal headaches" continued when incidents were about to happen and she experienced a multitude of events herself ranging from hearing footsteps and feeling gusts of wind from unknown sources to the appearance and disappearance of food as well as all the (by now) commonplace movements. Grosse had desired written communication from the entity or spirit and Mrs Hodgson found a note written on Janet's writing pad that said "shit Mr Grosse from Mrs Haylock". She had thought it was Janet's writing and threw it away. A further written message concerned keeping Mrs Burcombe away — Janet didn't like her. Grosse also believed that, on this occasion, Janet was responsible and he was disappointed that as soon as he was told to leave the room by Janet the pillow and bed clothes were thrown, which was inevitably suspicious.

On 9 November the first mention was made on tape of "growling" noises, which were to become very significant later on during the investigation and on 12 November the family was visited by some leading authorities on psychical research, namely Tony Cornell, Bernard Carr and Alan Gauld. Gauld and Cornell's presence was particularly welcome since they were to produce the highly informative book devoted to poltergeists two years later (Gauld & Cornell, 1979). Unfortunately, this case was not written-up in time to be included in their book. Frustratingly for them the phenomena did not manifest except when they were out of the room whereupon the pillow jumped and Janet was lifted out of bed and over Margaret before being dropped. With everyone present and amidst considerable laughter, Cornell clambered into bed with Janet and Margaret and then invited the 'entity' to move him out! Nothing happened and he withdrew. Once they were out of the room the activity started up again and Gauld set up some equipment with comments by Carr concerning "radiation". There were no significant results. An 'experiment' organized by Cornell involving water-filled balloons being placed beneath a bed, backfired when the balloons were discovered and thrown across the room leading to their bursting and water dripping through the ceiling into the downstairs room.

Later in the month the girls and Mrs Hodgson complained about having tickling sensations in bed and, on more than one occasion whilst he was sitting on one of the beds, John Burcombe was pushed off by an unseen "force". Events started to take on a more sinister turn from 13 November onwards. Janet became very "disturbed" and "violent" whilst what was described as being in a "trance". The combined forces of Mrs Hodgson, Grosse, Mrs Edwards (a family friend) and the Burcombe family all had difficulty in holding Janet down to stop her from hurting herself and they were unable to wake her up. The tape has disturbing footage of Janet who was "convulsing and banging her head on the headboard" and she was also said to be "... displaying a very strong grip like a grown man" whilst "... laughing, screaming, crying, yelling and kicking out". Grosse was kicked by Janet and she almost broke his thumb while she was "flaying around in bed". Nevertheless, Janet displayed natural behaviour during this turmoil notably by trying to keep her nightclothes pulled down to cover herself whilst frantically moving around. She then resumed strange behaviour by tying her socks together and imitating a Moslem's prayer position on the bed and rocking backwards and forwards. What followed was her being violently sick. Meanwhile Margaret had started "moaning" and was also "thrown out of bed" almost at the same time as Janet. After more screaming and "fighting" amidst what could only be described as pandemonium finally the activity calmed down and sleep was attained.

After these dramatic scenes the tapes do not reveal any further commotions until 26 November. In the interim period, Mrs Hodgson had talked about the difficulties both she and the girls experienced when her ex-husband visited with the maintenance money and, especially, when he brought his new girlfriend with him. The girls' relationship with their father was openly discussed, which did not appear to be very loving. Also, during the latter part of November, the author

John Fuller and his wife visited the family and discussed the phenomena with Mrs Hodgson. However, 26 November was another dramatic night with the photographer Graham Morris as well as Mr and Mrs Burcombe and Grosse present. Janet became hysterical again and started screaming and acting violently with "fantastic strength" during which time she accidentally assaulted John Burcombe. The doctor was finally called for and he gave her an injection of Valium that calmed her down leading to sleep. [Not recorded on the tapes that night was the taking of the photograph showing Janet perched on the radio and being held by John Burcombe.]

28 November contained further incidents and activity including a brush being thrown; the settee turning over backwards and the fridge door being thrown open so violently that it dented the door. Mrs Hodgson commented that events often seemed to happen at twenty-five minutes to the hour. Bedtime introduced the return of forceful action with Janet crying and biting Grosse's jacket. She also started to swear, which was to become very common later on. She exclaimed, "you are fucking hurting me". She was thrown out of bed several times and Grosse tried to demand the expulsion of whatever was affecting her.

Apart from a visit by the Brazilian mediums Luiz and Elsie Gasparetto who talked to the family and to Playfair (in Portuguese on the tape) the bedtime events for the remainder of November were similarly harrowing. Margaret was thrown out of bed several times; various items were thrown; and Janet was alternately crying or screaming. The commotion was also upsetting Billy. One strange conversation was recorded between the girls whilst they appeared to be asleep. Margaret spoke in a false-sounding monotonous voice, weirdly dramatic in its own way, saying to Janet "you mustn't sling that anymore or I'll tell Mr Grosse". The last part [edited] of the 30 November tape provides a feel of what was actually going on:

> ... Peggy Nottingham holding Janet down; MG narrates: "it's dead"; Janet: "no, it's fucking alive"... girls shouting [like a dramatic scene from a film or TV programme] ... Margaret awake; Janet crying and screaming uncontrollably; swearing ... Billy jumping around; Billy dreaming; chaotic ... Mrs Nottingham holding Janet down; "it's fucking alive"; MG says all gone; Margaret with fake voice; Janet says she's a witch; MG says their eyes are turned up.

December 1977

Outside of Christmas Day, Boxing Day and New Year's Eve there was hardly a single day during December that either Grosse and/or Playfair didn't visit the Hodgson household and make extensive recordings. A wide variety of occurrences happened during this time, which increased in variety and quantity and included frequent whistling, which the girls denied being able to replicate. On at least one occasion Mrs Hodgson and Mrs Nottingham believed they were actually doing it but without realizing it.

The month started with something of a curiosity since Janet appeared to be genuinely very upset by a door opening and closing by itself when she was alone "next door" and then being "thrown up the stairs".

However, the month's activities very quickly resumed, at least initially, with the common practice of flying objects; flying bed sheets; and Janet and Margaret being thrown out of bed.

Playfair quoted an account by Mrs Hodgson and a subsequent incident that he claimed was picked up "perfectly" by his tape-recorder, but the quality of the recording has deteriorated subsequently and it is difficult to hear.

> [Mrs Hodgson] ... It feels just as though there's a great big hand going like that ... You pinch me! You dare pinch me! You know you really are the limit. Now you go away! It's taken a fancy to my skirt ... [Playfair continues] ... my notebook jumped off the spot where I had carefully placed it, swished through the air and landed on the floor about three feet away ... This took place literally under my nose, in a strong light ... (Playfair, 2007, p. 108-109)

What can be heard on the tape is the sound of dragging followed by a "swish" as the notebook fluttered through the air and landed as if it had initially moved along a flat surface before taking off and falling.

All these incidents were witnessed by numerous people including Mrs Hodgson's ex-husband, but with Mrs Hodgson as the main observer. She again reiterated the headaches she experienced just before the activities started and that twenty-five minutes to the hour seemed to be a focal time for them. During this period the girls also started having simultaneous dreams/conversations/fantasies, which sometimes became quite crude with the emphasis on "dogs" and "shit". At times this was quite amusing to the extent that Grosse could be heard suppressing laughter in the background. When Grosse left the room, Janet was transported onto a chest of drawers in the room and Margaret was "thrown out of bed". Janet then became "violent" and it was difficult for the adults present to stop her from hurting herself as she thrashed around. On one occasion Margaret related in a monotonous voice whilst asleep "Wilkins died on chair downstairs". When she spoke of wanting to play a game called "Ten Ghosts" Grosse tried to coax the girls into attempting automatic writing while they were seemingly asleep, but the results were not conclusive other than that Janet wrote about "a ghost in the bedroom; it died in 1952; transistor radio has been buried at bottom of the garden".

5 December saw the arrival of David Robertson a physicist who had been asked to investigate the occurrences by Professor Hasted, the head of physics at Birkbeck College, and Hugh Pincott, a leading Council member of the SPR. Robertson set up measuring equipment, but the girls seemed to be in a playful mood. A laughing Janet was thrown out of bed and the adults were told to leave the room. The sounds of a bouncing bed were recorded and further girlish laughter with Janet accusing Margaret of "doing it". Other comments from the girls were "bugger off"; "it's great fun here"; miaowing sounds and a denial when Pincott and Grosse accused them of "messing about". Comments were made about being "bionic" and general childish and animal noises were made with Billy also joining in.

An altogether different atmosphere was achieved the following night (6 December) as Janet became violent again and Billy was upset by a dream he had experienced. Both girls were also thrown out of bed. Grosse admitted to being suspicious of some of the activity, but nevertheless consoled Janet when she was distressed at the implication that she was moving on purpose "like a gymnast".

As the upheavals showed no signs of abeyance, with Mrs Hodgson and Janet's permission, Playfair brought in a hypnotist to investigate. Dr Ian Fletcher was highly experienced in clinical hypnotism and a member of the SPR. In a relaxed hypnotised state Janet accused her siblings of "doing things deliberately", but she wouldn't tell her mother because she would "get the blame". She believed in ghosts and talked about being "OK" about Grosse and Playfair being there. After he had departed [the tape isn't clear here] the commotion started up again with bed shaking; Janet being thrown out of bed; Billy crying and wailing and persistent whistling. Grosse tried, in vain, to make communication with a knocking system of his own invention.

At 6:35 p.m. on 10 December "a growling voice heard near Janet" was recorded. This may have been the start of what was to follow when the 'Voice', or more precisely the 'Voices', became an integral and dramatic part of the investigation. Amidst the screaming and leaping out of bed, which had become commonplace, Janet started barking like a dog! This had occurred previously during the family's brief holiday when Janet had thought that Johnny was "barking" and he had thought she was – presumably this was some childish fooling around. Grosse asked for his name to be "barked" out and a number of barking sounds and names followed, which according to Margaret came "from under the bed". These included "Joe" and Grosse's name accompanied with "woof, woof", "fuck off", "shit" and one (or more) girls laughing. Grosse attempted to make verbal communication with the 'Voice' but was mainly unsuccessful as were his attempts to explore the whistling that had also become part of the activity. He did claim that at one stage whistling was heard near the tape recorder when no one was there.

The next visitors to arrive at the Hodgson household were John Beloff, Professor of Psychology at Edinburgh University and Anita Gregory, an experienced SPR member. Gregory asked several questions of the 'Voice' which was using different names ("Charlie" and "Joe") but the replies were mainly either abusive or of a growling/rasping/barking nature. She asked, "are you enjoying yourself?" and received the reply "yes, very much" followed by laughter.

Grosse was more successful with his cross-examination of the 'Voice' later on, but the replies to his questions were often absent or confusing. For instance:

> 'Voice' says it's Bill Wilkinson (age refused), lived in the house and was married with three children, but won't name them. Swearing follows.

> Grosse asks "how do you do your tricks"? Bed creaking, girls' laughter.

> 'Voice' says it steals money from the shop and has a dog present called "Goober the ghost". Bill now says he is 72 and says children are 16 and 18.

> 'Voice' wants Janet out of the bed and likes living in the house.

> Grosse asks further questions with either no reply or "fuck off". Violent bed-bouncing throughout.

GLP asks about jazz to which 'Voice' says "Scarlet Fever" – lots of girl' or girls' laughter and general laughter followed by "dog music" – fake barking, woofing and more laughter.

A singing session with Grosse, Playfair, Janet and the 'Voice'. ("Daisy, Daisy", "Don't Dilly-Dally", "Frère Jacques", "Oranges and Lemons" etc.). Grosse and Playfair are trying to get the 'Voice' and Janet to sing simultaneously. [This is not achieved on the recordings.]

Further swearing and childish statements "smacking bottom", "chocolate bars" wanted etc. followed by girls laughing.

Between the swearing the 'Voice' mentions it has "58 dogs to protect me"; "Joe" and ten others are mentioned; "I am Bill Haylock" and "I didn't die". The 'Voice' demands Grosse and Playfair must stay outside to "keep out all the germs".

After more bed creaking and general commotion on this occasion everything quietened down at around 2:00 a.m.

The next night it was the turn of Denise Burcombe to attempt a meaningful interview with the 'Voice' which had now become somewhat sexually orientated. The 'Voice' also identified itself as "Bill" throughout the conversation. After some initial swearing, "Bill" asked Denise to "kiss me" and said he was "on top of Janet" and "in the nude". He wanted Denise to take all her clothes off and, when she refused, swearing followed. "Bill" finally gave some details about himself:

> "I'm 72 years old ... I come from the graveyard at
> Durrants Park ... and all my friends ... we go to
> the pub ... and I used to live here ... when I was
> alive I suffered from blindness and I never had a
> dog ... and I died from a haemorrhage ... I'm Bill
> Wilkinson ... and I died 15 years ago ... and my wife
> died 4 years ago ..."

"Bill" then returned to sexually orientated matters and
talked about "bras and knickers" and "those things you
use", but he provided more information after Denise
persisted, saying he was very rich and had gold and died
of a haemorrhage and was "here" for quite a long time
and had three children Mandy, Wendy and George,
12, 14 and 18. He confirmed his name and address (the
Hodgsons') but added "I'm a naked man" and stated that
he had hundreds of friends some of whom he named.
His "best friend was David with brown hair and blue
eyes ...". Denise asked to come into the bedroom but
was told "No, fuck off" and so she was replaced by
her father John Burcombe who talked to "Bill" about
"God" who he ("Bill") claimed to be a "good friend"
and a "kind man".

A considerable degree of professionalism was provided to the case by the arrival of Grosse's son, Richard, a
solicitor who had agreed to interview Janet and record
his own observations, which he put into writing. [The
typed script is part of the 'Maurice Grosse Collection'
housed in Cambridge University Library as part of the
SPR collection.] Part of the question and answer session is printed below. [RG = Richard Grosse]

> RG: What happened to you when you died, just
> before and just after?

Bill: Just before I died I went blind and then I had a haemorrhage and I fell asleep and I died in the chair in the corner downstairs.

RG: When you had the haemorrhage were you in hospital?

Bill: No, no

RG: Where were you then "Bill"?

Bill: At home in the chair.

RG: What did you feel like when you died?

Bill: I cried and cried and wanted to come back and see my wife.

RG: And could you come back and see your wife?

Bill: If she was alive I could.

RG: Paul is holding a letter of the alphabet in his hand. Can you be very clever and tell us all what it is?

Bill: Later on.

RG: Why can't you tell us now?

Bill: He's a fucking swine.

RG: Who is?

RG: Where's your wife Bill?

Bill: Dead in the grave.

RG: Why aren't you with her?

Bill: Because I come back again.

RG: Why hasn't she come back again?

Bill: Because it's different; she's a woman I'm a man.

RG: Bill, I don't believe that.

Bill: Well I fucking well do.

The session finally came to an end because Mrs Hodgson wanted to go to bed, but Richard Grosse's report provided pertinent details of the background to the case and details about the house and people involved as well as the events that occurred. [The interested reader is recommended to read it in full.] Further conversation with Richard Grosse involved the hiding of Denise's money (30p) by "Bill" "under the radio downstairs" when no one was looking and "Bill" wanting Richard Grosse to give him a kiss. He was unimpressed with "Bill's" further comments about his being "handsome and goes to church on a Sunday ... he's a Jew and a vegetarian" and, after further swearing, "Bill" moved the conversation on to sexual matters again with comments about his girlfriend taking her clothes off and wearing "a bras and knickers". He also referred to Richard Grosse as a "Jewish rabbi ... that let germs in ... you wear funny hats and have funny hair" and were always "praying their heads off". Sometimes Janet's laughing can be heard on the tape. In the same session John Burcombe undertook some questioning of "Bill" and received the information that "Bill" was "on top of Janet" and invisible because he was a "G.H.O.S.T." that he was "in the nude" and was in the house to "see his wife". An argument followed as "Bill" insisted that he was not dead, but this was diverted as talk about a proposed visit by Matthew Manning on the next Saturday was mentioned. "Bill" said he would "put on a show" and that "there'll be a party". Manning had become quite a celebrity after TV appearances following his childhood experiences with alleged poltergeist activity and spirit contact. He led a luxurious lifestyle and later became noted for his psychic healing capabilities. After further conversations about trying to play the recorder and claims and counter claims concerning the validity of the manifestations, the adults decided to leave against "Bill's" wishes.

The arrival, on 14 December, of David Robertson and Hugh Pincott seemed to reinforce Janet/"Bill's" interest in sexual matters. After some initial confusion over the "Voice's" identity claiming to be "Joe Shifton" of "8 Amberside Crescent", the main "Voice" calling itself "Bill" returned to the scene. Despite the best efforts of Robertson and Pincott to veer "Bill's" questions away from sexual topics "Bill" persisted with comments like "take your clothes off"; "I'll pull your trousers down"; "can I see your bum" and statements about Robertson going to bed with his girlfriend. An intervention by Grosse caused "Bill" to respond to 'normal' questioning about where he was born which he guessed at and then started barking and singing. Grosse asked him to sing at the same time as Janet – "Scarlet Fever", "Daisy, Daisy", "Silent Night" and "Row, row, row your boat" – but "Bill" refused with "I know what you're fucking well up to". With the return of Robertson "Bill" returned to sexual themes wanting to see "a man's tinkle"; "men don't have babies like women … it comes out of their backside" and "they've got vaginas and not tinkles". Despite Margaret's telling "Bill" to "shut up" he repeatedly wanted to know "why do girls have periods?" and "why do they wear those things up their bum"? Robertson and Pincott explained as sensibly as they could and then had to continue with sex education concerning condoms, tampons, breasts and milk. During the times when sex was not "Bill's" focus he provided further information about himself – sometimes contradictory:

> "I'm 72 years old, I have three children Mandy, Wendy and Henry. Mandy is 12, Wendy is 16 and Jeffrey is 17; I come from Dewar's Park [?] and I have ten dogs who chase sixty-eight men" ["Bill"] used to go to a school at the top of the road about 68 years ago; had many friends, especially Joe [?] who had rich black

hair and a nice school uniform and so has Joe who has white hair; he used to play squash, which he wasn't very good at, and also played baseball."

The arrival of Grosse's wife and daughter did not encourage "Bill" to expand the available information about him in any meaningful way; in fact quite the contrary: "I've been around three thousand years" and answers to Grosse's subsequent questions were avoided. However, "Bill" did manage to explain how he had put a cushion on the roof and put a book "next door" by de-materialization and getting Janet to "float" into the room. The 'Voice' then switched from being "Bill" to "Fred" (Zebedee was also mentioned) and he offered Robertson money to tell him more about periods, which he declined. Grosse took over the questioning again and "Bill" expanded about his "sixty-eight dogs" which were six-foot tall Chihuahuas and then Labradors. Laughter and more slipper throwing ensued.

There was a destructive element to the next day's activity in addition to Janet leaping around. A microphone wire had been cut, much to Grosse's annoyance, and more spectacularly when he asked for "Bill" [?] to "throw the book straight out the window" a book was hurled at the closed window, which smashed it. During the subsequent taped angry conversation Margaret was heard to say "lying bastard" to Janet. Further frustrations were experienced the next night when a commotion was occurring in the girls' bedroom but the door appeared to be jammed from the inside, thereby stopping Robertson's entry. When, finally, the door was opened Janet spoke of "a white sheet going round the room" and the "bed drifted away". She claimed that they had de-materialized next door together and that the knob had come off the radio and started "flying around". During this event the investigators' tape-recorders had been tampered with.

> ... Bill had apparently been to work on our tape-recorders ... I found that one of my cassettes had one of its tabs cut off, which is very hard to do by accident, while another had either failed to record or had been wiped clean...Grosse's machine had been switched off in the middle of one of his tapes ... (Playfair, 2007, 140-141).

That same night Grosse tried an experiment with Janet by having her speak whilst her mouth was taped. The results were subdued when she was required to answer Robertson's questions. For the remainder of the evening Margaret spoke of the vision of "a little boy" who threw a stone at the Nottingham's [?] window and Janet's 'Voice' identity was "Charlie Brown" who very annoyingly kept repeating what everyone else was saying. [A common childish game.]

After starting the next night with a selection of animal noises and a rendition of "Old MacDonald had a farm" "Bill" admitted to breaking the window next door the previous night by throwing a stone at it. He then changed identities becoming "Charlie", "Fred", "Zebedee" and several other names. ['Charlie' seems to be quite a common name for entities. For instance, the name cropped up in a previous poltergeist outbreak investigated by the Rev. Michael Bunce in Grantham sometime in the 1980s. Whereas 'Zebedee' makes me remember a character in the children's TV programme *The Magic Roundabout*.] Grosse asked these entities to do "tricks" or speak simultaneously, but this did not happen. Further questioning revealed that the "Voices" could speak in different languages, however, some German counting was poor; there was no French and Robertson possibly mockingly asked for "Yugoslavian" which prompted no response. A brief song was started in Italian by "Bill", which evidently came from a record of one of Janet's friends and a song by Max Bygraves was monotoned [half-spoken/half-sung at one pitch]. Grosse conducted what he considered to be an important experiment to see if Janet could sing or speak when she had water in her mouth. However, after a few false starts, when she spat the water out or swallowed some of it, she could only manage a few grunts (as "Charlie") and "she nearly choked".

The tapes for 17 December also contain interesting material. Peggy Nottingham related finding one of Janet's books in her (Peggy's) bedroom when, according to her, it was not possible for any of the girls to have entered there. Matthew Manning visited the household and questioned Janet/"Fred" about the phenomena. The "Voice" was quite subdued in his company and could not provide any verifiable information about its origin. Manning did not appear to be very impressed by what he witnessed. By the next day, Grosse was understandably beginning to show signs of weariness at the constant activity and an experiment into metal-bending by the girls was a failure since a spoon could only be bent when it was out of the investigators' sight and a strong metal bar couldn't be bent at all, but was thrown instead.

The presence on 19, December of the sceptic Milbourne Christopher, who was also an excellent magician with a knowledge of ventriloquism, was likely to be revealing, since a positive outcome would have provided considerable impetus to the possibility of a paranormal origin for the phenomena witnessed. After a quiet start, various things were "flying around" including a slipper. The bed was creaking and, after the lights were switched off, the commotion started. The "Voices" identified themselves as "Ralph", "Claude", "Barney" and "George Mace" (who was still living) and the habitual "fuck off" was the response to questions from Lawrence Berger from the SPR. Whistling and growling followed from the "Voice" at a higher pitch than usual, including the England football chant often heard on the TV. Playfair's demand to "belt up" was responded to with "you're a sausage … double shit … get stoned", etc. Once the adults were out of the room, the drawer was emptied out and there was knocking on several surfaces. The recorder taped a curious episode when Janet crept out of bed after bedtime when she was discovered on the stairs by Christopher who produced a rasping sound [Playfair (p. 172) calls this "bellowing"] to which Janet said, "you've gone mad"! He believed that the "Voice" could have been an acoustical anomaly and he maintained that he had caught Janet in the act of being about to do something fraudulent until she saw him. He commented how Janet partially covered her mouth or turned her head away when using the 'Voice'; Lawrence Berger recalled how the "Voice" operated when Janet's mouth was taped but Christopher replicated the effect using a ventriloquist's technique.

The remaining days leading up to Christmas contained very few new phenomena. Grosse undertook further tests with Janet's mouth taped up or with water in her mouth, which, he believed, produced positive results. The various "Voices" seemed to be unable to speak when Janet's brace was in her mouth. A "Voice" calling itself "Jeffrey Prescilla" claimed to be using "energy" or "spirit's energy" and admitted to electrocuting the pet fish, which the family had once owned. Grosse asked whether the "Voice" might heal people, to which it replied, "yes". Another "Voice" referred to as "George" also came through Janet. [It should be mentioned that all the "Voices" were remarkably similar in their rasping, gruff tone.]

A disturbing and potentially dangerous series of incidents involved the curtains in Janet's room seemingly wrapping themselves around her throat on numerous occasions with such harshness that the curtain wire was eventually ripped apart. Grosse, Mrs Hodgson and John Burcombe witnessed the incidents, but Janet's hands were sometimes seen outside of her bed when the incidents happened. Grosse was more impressed when the mat beneath the double-bed was pulled out several times and a lamp was turned over without human contact. He felt that these episodes were impossible to do by normal means. The only other events were the attempted removal of a dressing gown and some slipper-throwing activity when no one was watching and a hanky that inexplicably landed on Grosse's head, which was also seen by John Burcombe. The remaining days of December were fairly uneventful compared with some of the previous activity. Janet's "Voice" identified itself as "Tommy" and "Fred" and Grosse used a "throat microphone" to try to distinguish Janet's voice from that of the various "Voices". He was hoping for the two voices to sound simultaneously, but that did not happen. The only other occurrence was Janet's kicking some of Robertson's equipment with the "Voice" statements "get that shit out" and "you fuck-arse" etc.

January 1978

January began with a very tense Mrs Hodgson relating at length the incidents from 31 December and early January, which included various objects "flying around"; a cupboard "rocking and knocking" and the "sideboard went over". She witnessed the Christmas tree jumping off the table and the decorations being torn down when nobody was close to them. "Tommy" announced he was doing it because he didn't like the machinery in the bedroom, which included a video recorder. [The results of the infrequent video-recordings never came to light, but they were mentioned in various scripts as being inconsequential.] Light bulbs were blown and Billy was hit on the head by a candle – he had a screaming fit and started to cry quite frequently, which may have been a precursor to his misery at having to go back to school after the holiday.

New developments recorded included a "Voice" speaking through Margaret claiming to be "a cheeky five-year old boy who died in 1812". She claimed that the "Voice" was coming through her neck with no movement through her mouth – Mrs Hodgson confirmed this. A knife allegedly started following Janet around, which she found understandably scary. After some childish conversation from Janet's "Voice" claiming to be "Fred Nottingham" a new identity introduced himself, through Janet, as "Cacheerio Ash" who claimed he was born in 1918 in Switzerland and died aged forty-five in a hotel in "Silver Street" in South London. Janet laughingly said he could be a dog or a cat and Grosse started to lose patience with what seemed to be a futile conversation. Both girls seemed to be enjoying themselves, judging by the amount of laughter on the recording. The renewal of the curtain activity 'attacking' Janet was making Mrs Hodgson very unhappy and she felt she had aged "since it all started" and she bewailed all the breakages that had plagued the household during this period. She said "It's not all trickery you know", but she admitted that there probably was the "odd trick". The curtains were subsequently taken down for safety reasons, whereupon the posters came off the bedroom wall and the bedcovers started moving of their own accord. Janet was also unhappy, believing that people thought it was her creating all the mayhem. Grosse consoled her stating that he didn't think she was doing things on purpose.

On 8 January Robertson and Berger were back at the Hodgsons' and Janet's "Voice" included sexual statements amidst the growling and swearing. Margaret was still producing a "Voice" and Billy also tried making similar sounds. Robertson described in detail how Janet could not have carefully tipped over a sideboard, which was full of books. There was a chaotic atmosphere at bedtime that evening with the "Voices" highly excited and abusive and the girls playing up as children can do. Grosse and Mrs Hodgson were both getting increasingly annoyed with the "filthy language" and Janet's rolling out of bed. John Burcombe accused her of knocking on the bed, saying "It's one huge joke", but Janet continued laughing and fooling around. Grosse in despair said, "You sound like a five-year old lavatory attendant" as Janet's "Voice" launched into further obscenities. Mrs Hodgson commented that "It never does anything when someone is in the room", but Janet said that she can't control it. Amongst all this activity the wallpaper could be heard tearing. Three more experienced investigators from the SPR were invited to visit the Hodgsons' home and duly arrived, namely Mary Rose Barrington, John Stiles and Peter Hallson. The latter felt "there's a sense of something in the room". They asked general questions but did not witness any direct phenomena other than hearing Janet's "Voice" saying "shit" a few times. After their departure the "Voice/s" (?) started croaking various pop songs and a TV theme ('Popcorn').

The tape for 14 January recorded new phenomena as well as the predictable "Voices". Mrs Hodgson related seeing the shadow of the lower half of a man-like an apparition, which was similar to an experience that John Burcombe had undergone. Writing had appeared on the toilet wall saying "shit" and, in red tape, the words "I am Fred", which Janet denied having executed. Mrs Hodgson claimed that the iron jumped "about three feet" with no one near it and that it had subsequently broken. Margaret reported that she saw an apparition staring at her from the airing cupboard. Later on Grosse insisted that there was "no lip movement" when Janet's "Voice" was talking – this was confirmed by John Burcombe – and Margaret was also tested. A rather humorous experiment ensued with Burcombe trying to get the "Voice" to say "bottle of beer" as opposed to "gottle of geer"! Attempted videoing was inconclusive, especially after several feet of undone tape "came down the stairs" whilst Janet and Billy were upstairs at the time.

Two days later on 16 January, John Burcombe narrated the history of the previous occupants of the Hodgsons' house. Mr Wilkins was evidently a quiet man who never swore and the people living there before him were the "Blackmans". The information, which Burcombe conveyed, contradicted some of the statements that the various "Voices" had made. Later that evening, Janet's "Voice" "Fred" was swearing so continuously that Mrs Hodgson became quite angry and, unusually for her, shouted at Janet. The following few nights contained an assortment of objects thrown, including Billy's slippers "dancing" behind Janet's headboard "for about ten minutes" and the regular "Voices" swearing and uttering obscenities. Grosse interviewed the girls separately about the "dancing slippers" but they gave contradictory accounts. A conversation between Janet's "Voice" and Grosse about someone claiming to have been "killed in the First World War" was terminated when Grosse pointed out that the dates that the "Voice" were giving didn't make it possible.

The "Voices" maintained their assault upon their listeners with crude words being sung to "All things bright and beautiful" and "There is a green hill far away". "Footsteps on the stairs" and "Row, row, row your boat" were also popular with them. The girls found this activity exciting to the extent that Janet's "Voice" complained about having "a headache" after yelling in a high-pitched growl and Margaret felt sick. Janet's "Voice" exclaimed "you won't keep me quiet" and continued talking about peanuts; a child's game; the toilet and sex comments and other obscenities. Despite the dubious nature of some of these happenings, Mrs Hodgson was still convinced that the children could not be responsible for most of the events that she witnessed. She related that a shelf came out and flew across the room when Janet was seated some distance from it and watching TV.

On 24 January, the American researcher Charles Moses visited the Hodgsons to make his own enquiry about the alleged phenomena. He asked many probing questions about the background of the family in a friendly and persuasive manner. Mrs Hodgson spoke about her financial problems and lack of a social life for both her and the children. Margaret's nerve problems of "three years ago" were also mentioned. He was brought up to date with the details of all the incidents that had occurred since the previous September. Janet's "Voice" announced "I'm up for it tonight" as it seems were the rest of the children, since Billy started to play about and a high-pitched growl and "Voice" conversed with Janet's "Voice". Moses took several photos and undertook a rapping experiment and an EVP [Electronic Voice Phenomenon] test, which involved Grosse and Robertson. He interviewed Janet at length, asking her about school, religion and her "Voice", which she said she couldn't do "to order", but it just came and then she got a pain in the back of her head. They admitted that their throats got a bit sore "after about two hours". Moses sent a tape of his opinion to Grosse after his return to Beverly Hills and he concluded that it was "without a doubt poltergeist activity". He believed that Mrs Hodgson's stress at the family's difficult circumstances, together with the children's adolescence, were main factors, but that the family's mundane existence was made more exciting with the various people in attendance. He felt that fakery was happening, whether conscious or unconscious, and that the girls would get tired of it in due course and things would settle down.

Another visitor was the BBC reporter Rosalind Morris who attempted to communicate with two "Voices", namely "George Mace" (who was still alive) and "Tom". She found that trying to imitate the "Voice" was "a strain on the throat" and the mentality of the "Voice" was like that of a small child. Daphne Pearce, a speech therapist at the North Middlesex Hospital, made further comments. She was invited to the Hodgsons' for an expert opinion and mentioned the use of the false vocal cord tone and dismissed the case for laryngectomy. She found the "Voice" to be a mystery and felt that sustaining the sound might lead to damage to the vocal cords. The next day Grosse, Robertson and John Burcombe prepared an experiment with a laryngograph to try to compare the differences in voice production between Janet's normal voice and her (on this occasion) "George Mace" "Voice". Grosse believed that the vocal sounds were "incredibly different". There was some playing up by Janet during this period of time; Billy was awake and Margaret complained about having a sore throat. Both girls were using "Voices" in conversation about "sixty-eight dogs", animal sounds and sexual matters. New names for the "Voices" were mentioned – "Stewart Surtan (?) and "Andrew Garner" who were said to be variously "a trapeze artist" or a fairground or circus owner. Another name "Stewart Carrick" was also mentioned. The conversation was very confused with silly jokes being told and assorted knockings such as the familiar da-dada-da-da da-da. The only other events were narrated by Janet and Margaret who claimed to see a fat man going into the bathroom. A pool of water was found on the toilet floor and there were toilet paper excrement smears on the wall.

February 1978

February's tapes started with Margaret's recounting what happened "last night" about the past life of "Andrew Garner" who said he was buried in their garden when he was ninety-two and was disturbed when digging happened there. Margaret's "Voice" then became confused and said he died twenty years ago and worked in a glass-blowing works and then, whilst laughing, the "Voice" said he was "murdered twenty years ago … crushed by a lorry by men". The name was then switched to "Hondy Garner" who was a comedian or a clown. Billy started "messing about" and the "Voices" became abusive. Mrs Hodgson genuinely believed that the girls were not just being abusive of their own accord and she talked about the children's childhood and unhappy times in the house and especially her sad memories about Johnny's being taken away – a broken family.

Grosse undertook numerous Raudive EVP tests where he invited any "entities" to communicate directly with the microphone. He claimed that the words "look at Tom" were spoken on his machine but a repeat test only recorded "walking across the ceiling". Subsequent tests were claimed to have produced quite startling results:

> He put his machine on the table, and said out loud "If there is any entity here, will you please communicate by speaking directly into the microphone"? A few seconds later came the reply, in a clear whisper. "No". [Playfair was also successful claiming he picked up: "Here I come" [and a faint] "hello".] (Playfair, 2007, p. 219)

There were a few problems with these results since the tapes did not make it clear that anything was being transmitted, which is often the case in EVP phenomena. Furthermore, the condition of the tapes does not enhance the identification of the alleged communication.

Mrs Hodgson related the appearance of a pool of water on the landing and on the toilet floor. There was also toilet paper on the floor, later, and excrement spread on the wall. Just before bedtime (8:40 p.m.) the settee jumped about five inches with Billy sitting on it which was repeated at 8:55 p.m. With the family having gone to bed, the "Voices" wanted to attract the adults from downstairs, namely Graham Morris, Grosse and Playfair. A "Voice" was heard saying "bang on the floor and they'll all come up" followed by "if you don't come up I'll smash the window" and "she's climbing on the roof". After Grosse went upstairs he asked Janet if she was asleep to which she answered "yes"! Both "Voices" then reverted to what can be described as "sex talk" – "Margaret wears those things" [tampons?].

On 8 February, some interesting facts were revealed to the Scottish TV producer David Martin. Mrs Hodgson gave details about George Mace – a friend of her ex-husband – and his connection with old furniture that had been removed from a house where a murder had taken place and been brought to their house. She had felt very low and depressed during the time just after Mr Hodgson had left and was facing financial problems also. She said that there was "activity" occasionally when the girls weren't in the house and that even Billy was now starting to swear. Grosse mentioned apports [objects appearing from an unknown origin] and "other" activity elsewhere, as well as an electrical malfunction which, he said, was reported by the recording engineers from Cambridge. He also commented about phenomena in Gary Nottingham's house next door where Gary's girlfriend had been pinched on the bottom when no one was near her. Martin tried to record some phenomena from the girls, but was not successful, other than a few sentences from the "Voice". The next day the "Voice" came from Billy, and Janet's "Voice" swore directly into the machine's microphone – "Mum needs a kick up the arse". Of perhaps more interest was Grosse's description of a fire discovered in a kitchen drawer found by Margaret where a box of matches was smouldering, and the discovery of "extremely smelly" urine on the bathroom floor.

At 12:35 p.m. on 10 February, Mrs Hodgson phoned Grosse from next door in desperation. The testimony was somewhat confusing, but it seemed that fires had broken out on the gas stove and the middle of the kitchen floor and on a mat there. A newspaper was smouldering and Janet pointed out that a washing powder box was in flames on the gas stove. A table had turned over; the settee had moved and Billy had been hit. Billy then took on the identity of "Dirty Dick" followed by Janet's "Voice". Grosse questioned Billy the next night about his "Dirty Dick" "Voice", which spoke about "digging the floor boards". When Grosse told Billy to try to stop the "Voice", Billy complained of a sore throat and started crying because he thought he was being accused of fabricating the "Voice" himself. Further incidents accumulated with Mrs Hodgson being hit on the head by a wall unit and butter being found in the middle of the floor. Grosse continued to attempt further Raudive tests and "Ali Bongo" was mentioned as a presence. Amidst these commotions, the TV volume was often very loud and members of the family were also heard playing/acting normally. "Voice" repartee with Grosse continued, which he believed to be discarnate because of the speed of its reaction to his comments.

A few days later, Janet described something that "came into her mouth like a rubber ball", which Margaret asserted had also happened to her and Grosse tried yet another Raudive test. Further incidents were related to Ivor Grattan-Guinness [SPR member], his wife and Anita Gregory who came to visit. Mrs Grattan-Guinness thought that, concerning the "Voice" phenomena, Margaret was "putting it on". They did not witness the multiple somersaults and bouncing around that happened with Janet and Margaret in their bedroom and the "Voices" conversation well after midnight that night.

Mrs Hodgson complained about the unannounced arrival of Bryan Rimmer and Graham Morris from *The Daily Mirror* at around 10:00 p.m. and Ray Alan, a ventriloquist and Clifford Davis, a TV critic. Ray Alan interviewed Margaret separately and she was very upset at not understanding his questions about faking the "Voices". She said later that she just nodded at his questions but didn't say she faked the "Voices" and that Janet had answered similarly. Evidently Alan had spoken to Margaret, comparing her situation with a belief in Father Christmas. Peggy Nottingham narrated that Mrs Hodgson later broke down in her house and felt suicidal since she was so upset about the previous night's visitors – the children were all crying. Peggy said that Neil Bentley had pressed her to obtain a confession and that he was a "bully".

For the remainder of February there were no new incidents, but some interesting information did come to light. Grosse spent some time in discussion with Professor Archie Roy, the President of the Scottish Society for Psychical Research and an experienced poltergeist investigator. Roy told Grosse that there had been similar cases to 'Enfield' in Scotland in past years and described the 'Sauchie' case from November and December 1960, which was investigated at length by the researcher A. R. G. Owen. Furthermore, tape recordings were also made of the phenomena which provided evidence of "agitated knocks emanating from a variety of apparent points of origin in the walls, floor and at times in mid-air." (Owen, *Man, Myth and Magic*, p. 2225) The parallels and similarities between the events were highlighted, which included banging sounds and the movement of furniture that was seen by multiple genuine witnesses. Playfair had a frank conversation with the children about "faking" and "tricks", some of which they admitted to. However, they assured him that they were not faking the "Voices". Janet said she tried to stop the "Voice" but couldn't. Playfair stated on the tape that he thought that "Janet may have suffered a sexual attack in Durrants Park graveyard last June where she was beaten-up quite badly". He also said that Mr Hodgson had been convicted of child-molesting when he was fifteen years old – an event which he had told the girls about. Playfair mentioned that Janet wanted to talk to Mrs Nottingham about her "problem" but no further information was made available as to whether this happened or was recorded.

March 1978

The recordings for March started with an important interview given by Hans Bender to Playfair. Bender was a professor in parapsychology who was responsible for the foundation of the *Institut für Grenzgebiete der Psychologie und Psychohygiene* in Freiberg. His most famous case was the so-called "Rosenheim Poltergeist".

He felt the Enfield case to be very interesting, but was less impressed with the "Voices". He stressed the need for a video-recorder and that detailed accounts should be categorised in terms of phenomena reported and ideally with multiple witnesses. They agreed that using a word such as "possession" was not useful and Bender felt that the family's attitude was "ambiguous" even if subconsciously, since a father-figure was being provided by Grosse's kindly and positive input into the family.

There was an absence of recordings for ten days since Grosse had been away, but Mrs Hodgson related that the movement of objects had continued during this time unabated, witnessed by the family and John Burcombe. She listed her experiences:

- knockings seen and heard by Janet
- a hand impression on a door
- drawers opening by themselves
- writing on the bathroom mirror with soap
- excrement in the middle of the upstairs floor
- a sugar bowl moving of its own accord

John Burcombe related:

- being hit by a swimming hat
- a box of Lego tipping over
- seeing Janet laughing at him from upstairs when she was downstairs
- seeing a man's shadow when no one was there

Perhaps of the greatest interest was the interview with Hazel Short, the crossing patrol lady who worked outside the Hodgsons' house. At around 11:50 a.m. on 17 December she saw a red cushion on the roof and books flying across and hitting the bedroom window from inside followed by a striped pillow. Janet was then seen going up and down in a horizontal position some distance in the air, which was also seen by Short's friend at the time. [A more detailed interview was given with Rosalind Morris in May 1978 – see below]. Grosse and Playfair undertook some measuring in the bedroom and found that Janet was bouncing twenty-eight inches from her bed. Playfair attempted this and could not succeed. He also tried to place a cushion on the roof as Janet had apparently done and again he was unable to do so.

Playfair was also instrumental in arranging the next visit of a medium to the Hodgsons. This was Gerry Sherrick, who was also a London taxi driver. He spoke at length about his spirit-guide "White Cloud" and told the girls that they were sisters in a previous life in York, where Mrs Hodgson was also living. He brought into the conversation witchcraft, ducking and burning at the stake and he also related his own experiences. Sherrick entered into a trance state and a somewhat noisy "White Cloud" gave a dramatic performance mentioning a female spirit who was pestering them and followed by other spirits. He then gave a reading with a variety of names and comments and recited a poem dramatically. At the end of the session a blessing was given.

Later on in the month, Mrs Hodgson related that a picture on the wall was seen spinning around on its own, which Grosse insisted was not physically possible. Paul Bannister, from the American *National Enquirer*, arrived but the recording of his visit was very confused since everyone was talking at once and it was therefore difficult to decipher what was being said. At bedtime Billy was acting disturbed and Janet's "Voice" was "grunting" and "spitting". Grosse became increasingly annoyed and finally tried another (unsuccessful) Raudive test at 10:20 p.m.

The final recording for (29) March was the "Cambridge Enfield Symposium" which consisted of a gathering of SPR members and other academics to listen to Grosse and Playfair's accounts of what was happening during this on-going investigation. After an introduction from the chair, Grosse started with a brief outline of the events and phenomena. He spoke about the police visit; the council and a medium being called in before the press were approached and the photographer Graham Morris was mentioned. Grosse related that he had first arrived on 5 September in Enfield and he reminded the audience that he had first spoken about the case at an SPR meeting on 8 September. He stated that over a thousand hours of investigation had happened onsite and that sixteen other SPR members had attended. There had been around fifteen-hundred incidents and about one hundred and forty hours of recording to date. Playfair then gave details of his own experiences there. Audience participation after their addresses included Professor Hasted who commented on the comparisons and contrasts between Janet's voice and her other "Voice".

April 1978

The first recording from April (9) consists of an interview by Grosse of John Rainbow a local tradesman (baker) who claimed to have seen some very unusual events in late December 1977. (He was unsure as to the actual date.) He had heard about the "business in the house" but thought it was a joke. His testimony taken from the 'Maurice Grosse Collection' was as follows:

On December 15th 1977, as a local tradesman doing my deliveries in Green Street, Enfield, I noticed a red cushion on the roof of number 284. At the time I was between one and two hundred yards away from the house. One moment when I looked there was no cushion on the roof and the next moment the cushion was on the roof. It just seemed to appear on the edge of the roof. As far as I was aware the windows of the bedroom upstairs were closed and as they opened outwards I don't think it was possible for the cushion to be thrown onto the roof.

On arriving outside number 284, as I serve the people next door in number 286, there was something very strange going on in the bedroom of number 284. The family in number 284 are not customers of mine and I only know the family by sight. Normally I would have just served the customer in number 286 and then I would immediately have left, but on this particular day I stood outside the house, as there was a considerable amount of noise coming from the bedroom in number 284. There were loud knocking and banging noises coming from the bedroom. As the cushion was on the roof it was a very unusual situation. I could see quite clearly into the room, for although one of the curtains was only partially drawn back, the other curtain was drawn right back and the window was clear. The windows were closed but the curtains were blowing back into the room as though there was a very strong draught blowing through the windows.

43

The order in which the events occurred were as follows. I saw this child, whom I now know to be Janet, well inside the room and in the first instance I saw her head bobbing up and down, just as if she was bouncing up and down on her bed. Then articles came swiftly across the room towards the window. They were definitely not thrown at the window, as the articles were going around in a circle, hitting the window and then bouncing off to continue at the same height in a clockwise direction. If the articles had been thrown they would have just hit the window and fallen down. The articles appeared to be books, dolls and linen articles. There were five or six articles and by their movement acted as though they were attached to a piece of elastic. They appeared to be travelling with considerable force and all the articles were going around at the same time. The child then appeared on two occasions floating horizontally across the room, and twice her arm banged forcibly against the window. I was frightened at the time that the child would come right through the window. At the same time as the articles were going around the room the curtains were blowing up into the room.

The whole episode was very violent and I was very upset and disturbed at what I saw. Very soon after the episode I was outside the house talking to someone about these strange events when Janet came out. She looked very vacant and certainly not like a child who had just been playing about.

Mrs Rainbow said that the episode had affected Mr Rainbow "quite badly". Grosse was particularly impressed with this account since it seemed genuine and Mr Rainbow had nothing to gain from recounting his experience and even risked ridicule for having told it.

The next day Mrs Hodgson related the movements of objects that had been witnessed, which included ball bearings from a game, marbles, bits of Lego, an armchair, kitchen table and cushion. Excrement was still appearing, on this occasion behind the taps, and there was further writing on the mirror. Both Mrs Hodgson and Margaret also spoke about seeing a floating childlike apparition in nightclothes and John Burcombe suggested the child's gown could have been a shroud. Mrs Hodgson mentioned that her brother had died at the age of five and that she was also worried about her son Johnny's return to the house from his boarding school. She added, "everything's going mad"!

Margaret described her visit to Chase Farm Hospital to see a psychiatrist, which was inconclusive. Evidently he said simply that the phenomena that she was experiencing would go away in due course. Grosse interviewed Mrs Burcombe and she related that she was with Janet and Margaret when the lamp on top of a cupboard fell over with a loud crash when they were "nowhere near it". An interview with Mrs Nottingham produced a graphic description concerning the toilet door opening of its own accord and a "pancake" like "stool" [excrement] appearing "hanging over the edge" after Janet had been there, which was very smelly and very dark in appearance.

As April continued so did the phenomena with an ever-increasing variety of manifestations. Shadows and apparitions were claimed to have been seen; cigarettes appeared; a perfume bottle smashed; "Bran Flakes" were "sprayed across the front bedroom" and still the

"Voices" growled, whistled and swore and the girls fooled around like children do. Grosse continued experimenting with Raudive tests and reported his own anomalous experience when a car parked outside his house was heard to have the engine running but with no ignition key in it.

The next visitor from abroad to attend the Hodgsons' household was Professor Miura from Japan. [Unfortunately no specific details were provided about him on the tapes.] He asked the family many questions about the incidents and the "Voices" and received answers that were consistent with what had been – and was still – happening there. Mrs Hodgson explained that at odd times the "Voice" would come from Johnny during the school holidays and that the "Voices" changed personality via the different children. Miura asked if the girls were worried about the "Voices" and they replied that they were not now, but had been at the start. They didn't like the scepticism of some visitors and were embarrassed when things happened in the shops. Mrs Nottingham made a strange comment that she had a fear of washing her hair because it often seemed to prompt phenomena. She said that Janet used to be thrown out of bed "fifteen times in one night". Grosse explained to Miura that he believed the poltergeist was people-focused rather than via the house and that amongst the "nonsense and rubbish" it seemed that something genuine was trying to be communicated. Mediums were discussed but they had produced different results with an emphasis on "an old woman". Grosse continued, "All poltergeist voices in the past have been deep, gruff voices" and very rarely anything else. He emphasized that the girls didn't always know what they were saying, but that the phenomena didn't seem to frighten them now ("it's a friend now") and they were sleeping better. With a degree of relief Grosse said, "It's better now than it was". He related that he used to have to go there in the middle of the night after they had called him, but it hadn't happened now for a number of months. In conversation in the car, Grosse told Miura that he didn't have much respect for psychologists and that he thought the girls were controlled by an outside influence, which could only operate with their own minds. Occasionally its own personality came through.

Before the end of the month, Janet related hearing noises and seeing an apparition of a man in braces and brown trousers and a ragged shirt who tried to scare her. He also had long nails and Margaret said she saw him too. He was about thirty-five to forty years old and standing near the bed for about five or ten minutes where he stopped her getting out of bed. She ran downstairs screaming; a fact which Mrs Hodgson confirmed.

May 1978

May's recordings start with Mrs Hodgson relating a number of incidents, but one humorous episode concerned Denise Burcombe's "missing pork pie". "I've got your pork pie" was written in soap on the mirror. Considerably less pleasant were the pools of urine and amounts of excrement that kept appearing. John Burcombe talked about the appearance of urine in the kitchen in a sausage shape, but Grosse didn't believe it was the children spreading excrement. Mrs Hodgson related further appearances of excrement and urine on the toilet seat and the floor with the stool being almost black in colour. She also revealed that she thought Mr

Hodgson might be responsible for some of the toilet activity. Grosse wanted to have it analyzed and Burcombe arranged for the urine to be analyzed at the hospital where he worked – it turned out to belong to a cat. Mrs Hodgson continued to list the events that were happening, mainly reading from her notes directly into the tape-recorder. Her list for the start of May was:

- the kettle lid flew off
- a plastic spoon bent
- fires in kitchen occurred
- milk bottles and Fairy Liquid was lined up on the floor
- crockery and cutlery were arranged when the children were not present
- a big puddle of water appeared
- the laundry basket jumped

She had also seen a small hand coming from Janet's bed and a big, old man's hand had been seen by Janet and Billy.

Some visitors from Germany (unspecified) arrived and asked about the phenomena. They were brought up to date by Grosse and the family with all the occurrences that had happened. Concerning the most recent events, Grosse talked about the "Voices" being "less crude now" and Mrs Hodgson felt it was a different person communicating. She also mentioned that the girls had recently been to the doctor and had been told that they were both fine. Soon after this, Grosse was in conversation with a "Voice" that told him his car had gone too fast. This was actually true since his car had recently malfunctioned through a mechanical fault. He was impressed that the "Voice" knew about this and didn't believe that he had mentioned it previously to the family.

On 11 May Hazel Short, the so-called "lollipop lady" returned to the scene for an interview with Grosse and the BBC 4 reporter Rosalind Morris. She recalled that in December 1977 she had passed by the Hodgsons' in the morning and noticed nothing unusual on her way to the school on a fine day. However, for her second duty of the day, at lunchtime, she saw a big, red cushion, on the eaves of the Hodgsons' house roof, which had not been there earlier. Margaret was standing outside the house. She asked Margaret if anything was wrong, since she had heard about the "goings on" there, but then she heard a heavy "thud" and saw a book followed by a pillow and then a book and pillow again hitting the closed window. She didn't see them drop to the floor. While she was looking she saw Janet bouncing up and down in a horizontal position about six times with her arms and legs flailing. There was only one curtain on the window, which was how she could see what was happening. After examination it was found that the bed was too low and didn't have sufficient spring in it to allow this bouncing to occur. She mentioned that Janet's body shape was "like a lazy 'Z'". Grosse thought the distance from the bed must have been about four feet because she cleared the first window frame. This frightened Hazel Short and her initial scepticism of what she had heard about the activity there was changed. She said that "her friend" saw it, too, but didn't want to have anything to do with it and kept away. She asked Margaret about the event and Margaret said that it wasn't unusual and that Janet was always doing things like that. Hazel didn't think it was being faked because she thought the Hodgsons were a nice family and didn't have the intelligence to set-up anything so devious.

Mrs Hodgson's list for mid-May again contained numerous examples of new phenomena (not exhaustive):

- a bucket came downstairs when Janet and Billy were both asleep upstairs
- Margaret's headboard came down
- during baking she heard an old man's voice whilst everyone was upstairs
- there was a line of wool that had pulled the light out when the family were all in the same room
- different things were flying across the room including batteries
- a tin of Lego "shot towards her"
- potato peelings shot across the kitchen
- a saucepan started spinning upside down
- glasses were flying around

John Burcombe told Grosse that he heard a voice swear at him in Woolworths and Mrs Nottingham found an ornament upside down in the house when no one was in and later Vic and Gary Nottingham heard knocking there. Janet saw an apparition of a man in a dirty white shirt and black trousers and an indentation was made on the bed. She levitated two to three feet above the bed and then almost up to the ceiling whilst lying down. She said she went right through the bed covers and landed on top of the covers.

There were some fairly angry exchanges about stone-throwing at this time between the Hodgsons and their neighbours. The children denied stone throwing despite the next door neighbours' complaint and observers couldn't find any children throwing them. Grosse agreed to help out and interviewed the neighbours involved. He interviewed Susan James from no. 286 and the Buckridges from no. 288. They both saw stones and dirt flying around and a milk bottle was also broken. Mrs Hodgson told them her children were inside and couldn't be throwing the stones, but the neighbours thought her children were probably too quick for her to see, especially with Johnny home at the time during the school holidays. The issue wasn't really satisfactorily resolved as to the source of the stone throwing. [Lithobolia (literally 'stone-throwing devil') has been known to occur in other poltergeist cases and notably the Cardiff Poltergeist Case investigated by David Fontana between 1989 and 1992.]

An interesting occurrence was recorded on 18 May concerning the tape recorder failure of Rosalind Morris during her interview of the Nottingham family earlier on. Grosse introduced and interviewed Mr Don Hitch – a sound recording engineer at the BBC in Portland Place. The specific jamming was caused by the tape, which had jumped off the feed spool and therefore stopped the recording. He explained that this had not occurred during seven or eight years of his personal experience in this way. He said it was not impossible but currently inexplicable.

The final recording in May (31) contains a number of varied events and incidents. Grosse continued interviewing people about their experiences and Mrs Hodgson related how Janet, Billy and even Johnny were "levitating". In Janet's case at one stage "six foot almost to the ceiling". Further stone and brick throwing were discussed and Mrs Hodgson related that stones kept flying around her at the cemetery when nobody was behind her – some were fast and some were slow. There was some general fooling around and Billy was caught intentionally jumping out of bed.

June 1978

June started in much the same way as many of the previous months had with a variety of incidents. Mrs Hodgson reported that she felt her bed was being lifted and she heard "scratching" sounds; the dressing table jumped sideways three times; a chair moved by itself followed by a sighing sound being heard; and a door opened and closed by itself. Johnny was at home at the time and he was hit by a furniture drawer coming out. Grosse narrated that some Tupperware items flew across the kitchen when Janet wasn't near them. There was "more activity upstairs" described by Mrs Hodgson and Grosse with a return to articles being thrown frequently. An unpleasant spate of spitting seemed to be happening – denied by everyone as the perpetrators – and excrement was found on a flannel and in the sink. In a discussion about Janet, Mrs Hodgson stated that she thought Janet might be doing things, but without realizing it … as if she was possessed by a spirit. Grosse was unhappy with this interpretation and favoured a hidden or split personality syndrome. He couldn't answer for the "paranormality" of it. Once again the idea that Mr Hodgson may have been the root of the problems was debated. Mrs Hodgson was afraid for Janet who was now starting to rock backwards and forwards and rubbing her hands together. (A well-known sign of stress in some individuals.) A few days into June, when Grosse and Robertson were present, Billy and the girls were all speaking with the "Voices" and particularly from Billy whose "Voice" was higher and speaking more childishly than the others. "Baa, baa black sheep" was intoned by the "Voice" but with the substitution of crude words. Robertson related that a tablecloth was thrown over him when the girls couldn't have reached it and a chair was moved in his presence. Other items moving included the table lamp wire and a magazine. An argument broke out when Mrs Hodgson accused one of the children of throwing something, which was hotly denied. Margaret accused Janet of lying saying "I caught you out".

On 16 June, Ed and Lorraine Warren, the American self-styled paranormal investigators and demonologists, visited the Hodgson family where they interviewed John Burcombe, Grosse and Mrs Hodgson. The taped event was somewhat confused by a simultaneous phone call occurring from a female reporter for a live show. Different dimensions were mentioned and Grosse said the source of the activity might be from "living people", but he didn't rule out a "discarnate source".

A few days later, Grosse interviewed Gloria Sutton, who was Gary Nottingham's girlfriend. She related that she had had her bottom pinched when she was alone. She had heard a rustling noise and a knock on the door, but when she turned round there was no one there, which scared her since she thought it must have been Gary playing a prank. He also interviewed Margaret about pulling the plug out of a video recorder, which she had felt compelled to do after Janet's "Voice" told her to.

July 1978

Mrs Hodgson was worried about Billy because he was moaning in his sleep and he was afraid to go to sleep because he thought the house was haunted. John Burcombe reported that Billy said to him "why don't you fuck off" in the "Voice" and he claimed that the door opened by itself when no one else was present. Workmen had been called into the house to inspect the plumbing, but could find nothing wrong with it. Mrs Hodgson reported many more incidents including a child's voice laughing being heard from the kitchen and a strong windy draught being felt. Vic. Nottingham related an incident involving a key that went missing in what he believed to be impossible circumstances. [It eventually turned up.] He said his brother was now too scared to visit them. Grosse interviewed Mr Richardson (Mrs Nottingham's father) about a metal dish that he saw levitate. He said that although he didn't believe in the phenomena beforehand, he most certainly did now.

Towards the end of July, Janet was admitted to the Maudsley Hospital for tests, which were not recorded on audio-cassette, but she did say that nothing happened there because there was no power built up from other people and Mrs Hodgson provided the details of the conversation with a doctor. She believed that Janet was better when she was not at home and had returned to her normal self like she was before all the trouble started.

The only other incidents recounted were lighted tissues appearing in the kitchen with a "Voice" saying "I did that" and a toy and door handle moving on their own. Mrs Hodgson related that her skirt was pulled and she was tapped on the shoulder and she heard an old man's voice as well as a "raspberry" being blown at her. When she was out shopping with Johnny he fainted, which caused some turmoil, but it was probably caused by physical ailments. Grosse was particularly interested in the fire phenomena since he was also concurrently investigating another poltergeist case (the "Spring Case") that involved similar occurrences. [The details of this case can be found in the SPR archives.]

August/September 1978

During August the activity quietened down whilst Janet was ensconced in the Maudsley Hospital. Grosse received a phone call from John Burcombe and Mrs Hodgson, relating an incident of everyone being in the kitchen when the sideboard went over and then Mrs Hodgson felt pushed. Margaret also witnessed activities in the kitchen and being hit on the head and Johnny claimed not to feel well.

By the middle of September, Janet was back from the hospital (she had been there six weeks) since Mrs Hodgson wanted her back. The hospital found her to be "quite normal". Mrs Hodgson disclosed that "we had things happening when she was away" and she spoke of unknown whistling and an unexplained indentation on a pillow. After Janet's return, knocking was heard and Margaret saw a "big fat man" in the bedroom making faces at her. Excrement and water was found on the floor again. Janet claimed to see someone sitting in an armchair like a shadow and she also heard strange noises like a dog, which frightened her, in the bathroom as well as outside.

October 1978

Although the activity was abating, it had far from dis-appeared and Playfair arranged the attendance of the Dutch medium, Dono Gmelig-Meyling, recommended by his Dutch friend Peter Liefhebber. They duly arrived and the medium claimed that his task was to dispel the bad energy. Mrs Hodgson related all the events that had happened and Dono claimed that he had an out-of-body-experience (OOBE) at Enfield where he saw a twenty-four year old girl and "something with her head". He felt tension and something in Grosse's aura with a strong psychic influence. He spoke of a foreboding sensation and negativity in the house. The available tape provides details from Playfair (at his ho-tel) of Liefhebber's description of Dono and Grosse's conversation. He said that the medium told Grosse that it was his daughter, Janet, that was "haunting" Enfield. Dono believed that Grosse was integral to the case via a "twenty-four-year-old girl". Playfair stated that he could not believe that Janet Grosse was the cause of the disturbances and neither did he believe that it was all finished. He expanded on Gasparetto's visit and his own experiences in Brazil. Grosse, on the other hand, was said to be very impressed with Dono. In theory, at least, the case seemed, now, to be over.

Interlude

The audio-tapes belonging to Playfair finished with the above examples. However, the Grosse tapes continued sporadically as he returned to Enfield to make contin-ued enquiries. One of the problems with these tapes was their erratic chronological definition. [Hence the use of a question mark after the dates provided.] Dates are sometimes incorrect or not specified. The content was also very difficult to decipher at times because of faulty recording or tape deterioration. Fragments of some of Grosse's other cases were also included on the Enfield tapes, which are interesting, but have no bearing on the case in hand. They have therefore been excluded here.

April 1979?

Mrs Hodgson related that a door handle turned by itself; she heard knocking and then a bang as the door shut while the children were seemingly asleep. Further incidents included the kitchen scales moving up and down the wall and a key turning of its own accord in the back door. She said she was more scared now than before and she talked about "Mr Wilkins" who died there of a heart attack and went blind. She heard a disembodied male voice as if someone was behind the wardrobe, which then fell on the bed, which hit Billy [?] on the foot. Vic Nottingham recounted further mysteries concerning a pile of pennies that appeared on his bed after he had questioned Gary (his son) about them. More information was given about Bill Wilkins, and Denise Burcombe related her story about seeing a shadow at the door. Janet and Johnny were recorded illustrating their "Voices" with Grosse's assessment.

For the remainder of April, Mrs Hodgson listed the following incidents:

- a chest of drawers jumped of their own accord whilst everyone was in bed

- things seemed to come through the bedroom wall, flying around (bottles, tubes and glass beads)
- the top came off some hand cream and spread across the bed "a thin line of cream about four feet long"
- Johnny's bed jumped up and down
- a book flew across kitchen
- stones landed from unknown sources
- a table moved and the settee moved several times
- an apple flew across the room
- a bottle of bubble bath and other bathroom items came "through the wall"
- batteries appeared from nowhere

Janet related that a boot came through the door at breakfast time and that the teapot disappeared; bread slices were flying around and the sugar was knocked over. Grosse asked about the possibility of the children misbehaving, especially Johnny while he was there, but Mrs Hodgson assured him it was not possible, apart from perhaps the odd bit of mischief from Johnny. Grosse had a washing up brush thrown at him from the kitchen at "great force" and he witnessed a scarf moving up in the air off the sideboard.

May 1979?

According to the tapes, Grosse made only two visits to the Hodgson household in May (10 and 20) and this was to receive the testimonies of the Hodgson family, the Burcombes and the Nottinghams rather than to record actual events. Mrs Hodgson talked about a mess made by a tube of hand cream, but Johnny was present at the time and, what's more, things were found concealed in Billy's bed. They agreed that Johnny was probably responsible for some incidents and that it was quieter when he wasn't around. Janet's "Voice" came through now and then and six floating pairs of knickers allegedly followed her into the bedroom. Vic Nottingham and John Burcombe both related events from the past.

14, August 1979?

John Burcombe related that the Warrens had "arrived out of the blue" early in the morning and taken loads of photos and that the children had become very excited since the girls were going to be taken out for a meal at a Wimpy Bar – but not the boys. Mrs Burcombe was very unhappy about it and Mrs Hodgson was also annoyed at the Warrens' constant interviewing. They talked about making money and, it was said, "they are trying to capitalize on the case". According to Mrs Hodgson, the Warrens appeared to be against Grosse and Playfair and "they were encouraging it" [the phenomena]. Janet threw some tantrums and Mrs Burcombe said, "half the "Voices" were fake". There was writing on the wall, quantities of water from unknown sources, bangings and knocking on the wall and a heap of dead flies on the mat, which Billy might have perpetrated. John Burcombe narrated that an ashtray disappeared and appeared when no one else was there and that there was "a lot of activity" after the "Americans" came.

12, October 1981

This tape provides details of an interview by Grosse with Charles Kennedy who was acquainted with Bill Wilkins and was allegedly the main "entity" or spirit during the case. Kennedy described him as a respectable and generous man who didn't use foul language. He was always clean and tidy and died at around eighty (later changed to seventy-two). He liked dogs and the names Charlie, Fred and Bill Haylock meant nothing to him. Mrs Wilkins died of throat cancer in hospital. Grosse played the "Voice" recording and Kennedy thought it was the character of the man he was and that he would have liked songs like "Daisy, Daisy".

An interview with Terry Wilkins in 1997

Grosse was contacted by Terry Wilkins, the son of Bill Wilkins, who agreed to be questioned about his late father. Terry said, "it doesn't sound like his father, who was a quiet man". He mentioned that another man had died in the house earlier, but Grosse didn't recognize his name. The age of death given on the tape by the "Voice" was wrong which, Grosse said, "is understandable". Terry talked about the circumstances of his father's death, which was not a heart attack, but he did go blind before he died. Grosse provided further incidents from the investigation, but Terry didn't think it sounded like his father, but more like a child talking. Grosse suggested that it might be something impersonating Terry's father who also didn't sing or whistle particularly. Grosse said he thought the personality would be different from Terry's father.

Conclusion

Thus comes to an end the details of the recordings made by Grosse and Playfair, which are housed in the audio archives of the SPR. Their digitalization – when possible – ensures that further deterioration will be minimalised, but some of the tapes were too far gone to be resurrected. Their advantage over the written script is that they convey information that the written word can sometimes fail to identify, especially when multiple conversations were being held simultaneously and with tones of voice implying different emotions. With the absence of detailed video-recordings and round-the-clock closed circuit monitoring that the twenty-first century would provide, the tapes are probably the best documentary evidence of the veracity or otherwise of the alleged paranormality that occurred during the Enfield Poltergeist Case.

CHAPTER TWO

The Report of the Enfield Poltergeist Investigation Committee (EPIC)

Introduction

At a Council meeting held on 25 May 1978 an agenda item was discussed that led to the formation of a committee to collect and collate evidence and experiences from all possible sources concerning what became known as the Enfield Poltergeist Case. The committee consisted of Mr J. W. Stiles (Chairman), Miss M. R. Barrington, Dr P. Hallson and Dr H. Pincott. They met on at least fourteen occasions and drafted a letter, which was sent out to thirty people who had visited the scene of the disturbances from whom they received twenty replies.

In addition to this, Guy Playfair made a detailed report of his own describing events that had occurred there up to 10 December 1977. The subsequent report was expanded and Playfair was joined by Maurice Grosse who provided verbal and photographic evidence.

The report was presented in several sections:

- The Playfair report (see previous paragraph).
- Clarification/elaboration of incidents based on questions put to Grosse and Playfair.
- Reports by visitors to the Hodgson establishment as a result of letters sent to them by the committee.
- The committee's interviews with local witnesses.
- General conclusions regarding the witnesses, investigators and phenomena.
- The committee members' own views.
- Appendices.

Confidential papers were filed separately and the committee admitted to not having examined ALL the photographic material. It also admitted to having "not undertaken *any study of the audiotapes* [my italics] except in relation to certain incidents".

The Playfair Report

The Playfair Report included the background to the case; the people concerned; the incidents; and their own opinions and comments. (Much of this appeared in Playfair's subsequent book *This House is Haunted*.)

Playfair and Grosse provided a very useful list of categories of incidents which were either "observed by or reported to" them. They claimed not to have witnessed events only in nos. 7, 9 and 10.

1. Percussive sounds.
2. Throwing of small objects.
3. Movement of furniture.
4. Opening and closing of doors and drawers.
5. Interference with bed clothing.
6. Appearance of liquid and solid substances.
7. Apparitions, both partial and total.
8. Levitation of persons.
9. Physical assaults.
10. Presumed passage of matter through matter.
11. Psychological disturbance.
12. Automatic writing and drawing.
13. Automatic speech.
14. Disembodies voices.
15. Equipment failure.
16. Outbreaks of fire.

During the course of their report, Grosse and Playfair claimed to have made approximately one hundred and eighty visits to the house in Enfield, including twenty-five all-night vigils, making an equivalent of more than one thousand hours. They also reported some one hundred and forty hours of tape recordings up to the time of writing their report in June 1978.

They presented many written reports to substantiate the veracity of their claims. Of particular importance to them was the report of WPC Carolyn Heeps who attended a disturbance there:

On Thursday, 1 September at approximately 1:00 a.m. I was on duty in my capacity as a policewoman when I received a radio message to 284 Wood Street [address used in report to avoid disclosure of actual address], Enfield. I went to this address, where I found a number of people standing in the living room. I was told by the occupier of the house that strange things had been happening during the last few nights [Playfair interposed that he thought this was a mistake for "hours" instead of "days"] and that they believed the house was haunted.

Myself and another PC entered the living room of the house and the occupier [actually Vic Nottingham] switched off the lights. Almost immediately, I heard the sound of knocking on the wall that backs onto the next door neighbour's house. There were four distinct taps on the wall and then silence.

About two minutes later I heard more tapping, but this time it was coming from a different wall; again it was a distinctive peal of four taps. The PC and the neighbours checked the walls, attic and pipes, but could find nothing to explain the knockings.

The PC and the neighbours all went into the kitchen to check the refrigerator pipes etc. leaving myself and the family in the living room. The lights in the living room were switched off again, and within a few minutes the eldest son pointed to a chair which was standing next to the sofa. I looked at the chair and noticed that it was wobbling slightly from side to side.

I then saw the chair slide across the floor towards the kitchen wall. It moved approximately three to four feet and then came to rest. At no time did it appear to leave the floor. I checked the chair but could find nothing to explain how it had moved.

The lights were switched back on. Nothing else happened that night although we have later reports of disturbances at this address. (Signed) Carolyn Heeps (10 September 1977).

The possible lack of light was resolved by Playfair stating that the room was still "being lit by the street lamp outside and by light coming through the open kitchen door". Prior to Grosse's first visit to the house on 5 September it was stated that a number of "council officials, police officers, two clergymen, a local self-styled medium, and others" visited. It was also claimed that Mrs Hodgson was told that she could be re-housed if she wished, but she declined this offer.

Further testimonies were included in the report including that of the photographer Graham Morris who stated that after he had developed the film he "found a small hole in this negative, as if made by a hypodermic needle. Neither he nor another experienced Fleet Street professional subsequently consulted could recall seeing a similar mark on a negative". Concerning the actual incident Morris stated: "I saw the Lego piece flying around, and I was hit on the head by a piece while I was attempting to photograph it in flight. I had a bump on the forehead after the incident." The incident was witnessed by Mrs Nottingham who reported that, "I clearly witnessed the flying Lego pieces. I saw the Lego that hit Graham Morris fly through the air from the window area at a height of about six feet." She mentioned that another "lump caught my husband on the elbow".

Other reporters and photographers were also in attendance, namely George Fallows and David Thorpe, both from *The Daily Mirror*. They reported that in the early hours of 8 September 1977:

> We were standing back from the door on the landing and were looking into the bedroom at the books on the mantelpiece. There were three books and the middle book had been found twice before on the floor. The girl Janet became restless in bed and the restlessness seemed to preface the manifestations we were trying to witness. While looking at the book, we heard a bang and Thorpe saw the chair in a toppling movement as it moved about four feet from its original position. Mrs H. [Hodgson] in the next bedroom was also restless at this time. Mrs Grosse immediately examined the girl and said she found her in a deep sleep.

Grosse found her eyes "upturned after he had forced her eyelids open. Janet showed no reaction to this handling of her eyelids".

Tape-recording was not used in the earliest part of the investigation, which makes written testaments necessary, which can be fabricated or, in a worst-case scenario, be untruthful. One early incident, which was reported by Mr Richardson, occurred when no one was close by:

> I sat down on the settee while Janet went over to the fish tank. She put some rocks in the tank that Mr

Grosse had brought for it. She replaced the cover on the tank, and then walked into the kitchen. A few seconds later, while Janet was still in the kitchen, the top of the tank landed on the floor about four feet away from the tank. Janet heard the noise and came back into the room and said, "Well, I didn't do that did I"?

Grosse later "tried to put the top of the tank in a position where it would slide off under slight vibration, but have been unable to do so".

Playfair arrived at the household for the first time on the evening of 12 September and departed at 12:20 a.m. From his own log he recorded:

> To test Janet as source of deliberate object-throwing, I whispered loudly to GM [Graham Morris] after some minutes' silent observation in her bedroom, "She's asleep, we can go down now". As previously arranged, GM left the room and went downstairs while I remained seated on the other bed. As soon as GM had gone downstairs, Janet's head popped up. On seeing me, she dived under the sheets again.

Graham Morris obtained some specialist remote control equipment to try to catch any phenomena firsthand. He placed "three motor-driven Nikon cameras on tripods so that by pressing the cable release, the whole of Janet's room could be photographed. His signed statement reported that:

> ... three of my electronic flashguns developed faults simultaneously... As soon as they were set up in the bedroom, they started to drain themselves

of power. ... The equipment ... had been in my possession for more than two years and none had ever given any trouble. They are generally considered to be foolproof. ... After leaving the house, all three resumed normal functioning. I am unable to explain this episode.

On the evening of 23 September a team from Pye Business Communications Ltd, Cambridge visited, at Grosse's request, with infrared and ultraviolet recording equipment. It was set up in Janet's room between 9:30 p.m. and 1:00 a.m., but only recorded Janet sleeping. They agreed to return the next night, but initially the machine would not operate. Mr R. H. Denney (chief demonstrator) and Mr David Annett (product manager) later stated:

> ... When we attempted to turn the machine on, it would not load, and therefore we could not unload it. We tried numerous times but without success. We eventually had to dismantle the machine from outside to get to the mechanism, and finally found that the tape itself had dropped underneath a guide pulley and had jammed that pulley onto a pin on which it normally rests. It needed considerable force to separate the two parts. It is not impossible for a fault like this to happen, but it is extremely rare. Neither of us has ever come across this fault before.

Once the equipment was working normally, Janet was filmed sleeping peacefully until 12:45 a.m. when they departed.

During the subsequent months, numerous other events and testimonies were recorded in the Playfair report [the full report is housed in the library of the SPR in London and another copy is held at Cambridge University Library, Cambridge]. Grosse and Playfair attempted to replicate some of the phenomena to see how difficult it would be to fake the activity. Numerous experiments were undertaken, including trying to communicate with the raps and Raudive-type EVP tests. On 15 October, Playfair witnessed events himself which left him with no uncertainty as to the authenticity of the activity:

> Something was going over in the kitchen as I came in... the other red chair in LR [living room] went over while I had Janet in view. ... Even better was also to have Janet in full view as K [kitchen] table went over ... (to Janet) Well, you didn't do that one!

One of the major witnesses cited in the Playfair report was John Burcombe. Both investigators found him to be level-headed and not prone to fantasies. However, he did appear to be considerably alarmed by his possible experience of an apparition on 15 October 1977:

> I was in Mrs Harper's [Hodgson's] house last night (15 October) when I saw this light. It was the equivalent, I would say, of approximately twelve inches vertical. It looked like a fluorescent light behind frosted glass, which burned fiercely and gradually faded away ... It was, I would say, roughly waist height ... I was bloody petrified. I'd never seen anything like it and the feeling that I had was one of fear, like there was somebody standing right by me and watching. I've never known such a feeling in my life ... I was standing at the bottom of the stairs looking up. Now,

there were no doors open and there was no way any light could have shone in from outside.

The "flying box incident" was one that Grosse was particularly fond of quoting since he and others felt it unlikely that "better evidence of this type is likely to be obtained". The activity was captured on tape [see November 1977] and followed a line of questioning being undertaken by Grosse using rapping for communication. Having asked "are you having a game with me"?

> ... the cardboard box full of soft toys and cushions in the corner of the bedroom beyond the head of the bed rose from the floor and flew in a straight line directly at MG [Grosse], hitting him squarely on the head. GLP [Playfair] was standing behind the open door and was able to witness the fall of the box to the ground. The authors are thoroughly satisfied that the box was not thrown by any of the Harpers [Hodgsons].

The box evidently travelled "about eight feet" and when the authors, and later a BBC television film unit, attempted to stage a reconstruction they could not replicate it with any ease by throwing it in a normal manner.

Playfair reported that six SPR members attended the Hodgsons' home on 12 November 1977, including Alan Gauld, Bernard Carr and Tony Cornell. He summarized their actions in the report and mentioned the equipment that was used and their behaviour. [More details can be found under the section 'The Committee Members' own views.] However, Playfair was rather aggrieved by Cornell's actions and wrote:

> Mr Cornell carried out an experiment involving balloons filled with water, which made a good deal of mess and caused the family some annoyance. He also had a talk with the girls, which left them both under the impression that they were being accused of playing tricks. Mrs Norton [Nottingham] later reported that after the departure of Gauld, Carr and Cornell, the girls had come to see her considerably upset and in tears, saying that they had been falsely accused of "cheating".

The previously mentioned episode of Janet's hysteria and the subsequent visit of a doctor [see tapes 26 November] were expanded in the report since they were not taped. Playfair detailed her trance being repeated the following night (27 November) and that the doctor was called again. The next morning she was taken by ambulance to Chase Farm Hospital. Grosse's script describes the difficulty of the situation. Grosse, John Burcombe and Mrs Hodgson met up with a psychiatrist at the hospital who was told of the problems encountered. It was evident to Grosse that he would not accept the possibility of "paranormal activity" and he said that "we should avoid getting Janet entangled in any type of hysterical situation whatsoever". Grosse then related that John Burcombe was told suddenly that Janet had to be admitted after Grosse had been told she was free to go. On 28 November she was given "a dose of Ativan" but, despite this, she "began another trance". The situation was getting out of hand and, with the efforts of the local National Health Service not being able to offer appropriate help, Playfair turned to his friends the Spiritist mediums Luiz Antonio and Elsie Gasparetto. The script here is useful since much of the recording was spoken in Portuguese between Playfair and the Gasparettos. [It is duplicated below from Playfair's notes.]

Elsie gave healing passes to Mrs H (Hodgson) and Luiz did the same for Janet, who made attempts to hit him. Then Luiz held her hand and sat quietly with her for about fifteen minutes, after which she calmed down. ED (Elsie?) and LAG (Luiz) then went upstairs for a private session, with LAG soon entering trance. This was interrupted by noises from below, where we found Janet off again in a fit of some violence.

At one point she got under the heavy wooden table and tried to kick it over, with me lying on it. She got it some way from the wall and then writhed on the floor with LAG hold[ing] her gently and talking to her in English, which he speaks, though not fluently, and Portuguese.

After kicking in a panel of the chest of drawers under the TV set, Janet suddenly began speaking unmistakable Portuguese, calling for "mamae" (Mummy) in just the intonation a Brazilian child would use … (With stress on the second syllable.)

By 6:15 p.m. Janet was (relatively) quiet, though moaning piteously and still asking for "mamae". Luiz, in Portuguese and English, said he was helping her; her mother was there if she went to look for her, and "she" must leave Janet's body.

By 7:00 p.m. Janet was sound asleep. She did not wake up until 8:30 a.m. (30 November).

Luiz told Playfair afterwards that there were several entities, "led by a very nasty little girl. Janet was a deep trance medium and must be trained and guided at once". Soon after this (30 November) Janet entered what Playfair described as "a relatively non-violent trance" during which she drew a woman with blood "pouring from her throat" (in red) with the name "WILKINS" written on it. He alleged that the previous occupant of the house was a Mrs Wilkins who had died twelve years earlier of throat cancer.

The alleged spoon-bending activity was also expanded upon in the report compared to what was mentioned on the audio tapes. These occurred in December 1977 when Playfair related;

> After breakfast I gave Janet a spoon and asked her to bend it. Watched all the time by Mrs H (Hodgson) she put it on the table, turned her head away and shut her eyes. It bent by itself on the table. I did not see this.

Mrs Hodgson claimed to have seen it bend and Playfair didn't believe that Janet could have bent it manually. Mrs Hodgson testified to Grosse on 10 December that she saw "two spoons bending as they lay on the sideboard", which was mentioned by Playfair in connection with the strain gauge used by David Robertson, which "apparently" gave positive results. It was a pity that Carl Sargent's visit in March was not recorded since it was alleged that he "carried out experiments with a PK meter".

Clarification/elaboration of incidents based on questions put to Grosse and Playfair.

Grosse and Playfair were frequently cross-examined concerning the statements made about their investigation at Enfield. Their answers to such questions mainly confirmed what had already been said. For instance, regarding the movement of the fish tank lid, Grosse repeated that it had landed "about four feet away". He said that he and Playfair could not "make the lid fall in this way" and that Mr. R. [Richardson] was supposed to have seen the lid go up in the air. Concerning the alleged movement of the refrigerator, Grosse confirmed that it was "heavy and difficult to move" and required "pushing" to move it back to its normal place. He also confirmed what had happened during the WPC's visit, namely that no one was in pushing distance of the chair and that its movement was upright and steady. "The WPC examined the chair and said that no one could have moved it".

Grosse provided useful clarification concerning the throwing of the box incident when he was hit on the head:

> ... he saw it coming straight at him. He had been kneeling down on the left (east) side of the bed, "talking" to the wall behind the bed, so the box must have come at an angle of about 90 degrees away from where he was facing. Billy was closest to him, Janet was closest to the box and Margaret was in the middle position. MG [Grosse] felt quite sure Janet could not have got to the box. She could barely reach it with her right hand, leaning well out of bed, and it would have required propulsion by both hands.

Playfair supported what Grosse said and mentioned that he saw the box hit Grosse, but not when it took off. The box was made of "floppy" cardboard and would have required two hands to pick it up. He further commented that he had been talking to the "entity" downstairs just prior to the incident and had said to it "Do you realize that you are dead"? Playfair challenged Janet's physical flexibility when he found the double bed up-ended against the wall. After he remarked to Janet that she "couldn't have done that" she put her knee under it and did "just that"!

Reports by visitors to the Hodgson establishment as a result of letters sent to them by the committee.

It will not be possible, here, to include the full testimonies of all the people who submitted reports to the SPR Committee and, once again, I would advise anyone wanting further information to consult the 'The Report of the Enfield Poltergeist Investigation Committee (EPIC)'. In addition to those presented below, reports were received from John Rainbow and David Robertson, which have not been included since their testimonies have already been presented in the sections on the recorded phenomena, as have much of what was reported by the local witnesses. Tony Cornell wrote a very detailed account of his visit, which has not been made publically available to date (2019). However, I possess a copy of this report and it is highly critical of the investigation. Cornell wrote that nothing that he had heard about Enfield or seen there convinced him that it was "the case of the century". Although he liked Playfair and Grosse as individuals and had "no doubts about their sincerity or honesty", he was "far from impressed with their apparent preconceived ideas and conviction that it was a poltergeist case". He felt that they interpreted everything that happened as resulting from some form of "discarnate intervention". He thought that this attitude could produce "biased and misleading accounts", which would be detrimental to making a "balanced assessment" of the case.

Mr. John Stiles

John Stiles visited the Hodgson household on 13 January 1978, with Mary Rose Barrington and Peter Hallson, all prominent members of the SPR. The family was present, excluding Maurice Grosse and John Burcombe who arrived later. Most of the time was devoted to Mrs Hodgson relating the various incidents that had happened. He was impressed by "all those questioned" being "clear and detailed" and found Mrs Hodgson to be both "sensible and sincere". He heard the "Voice" "coming from the vicinity of Janet – an unpleasant sleazy masculine voice uttering various obscenities". He found it surprising, but believed "she could have produced it" and evidently Janet had spoken about having a sore throat after "prolonged manifestations of the "Voice". Stiles then commented on what Barrington and Hallson experienced there and added that he felt that Janet could have wrapped the curtain around her own throat when this phenomenon happened... as it frequently did. He concluded, "In my opinion all the "phenomena" which occurred during this visit could have been and probably were produced by Janet, knowingly or unknowingly".

Mr. Francis Huxley

Francis Huxley's report was dated 21 February 1978 and it was implied that he visited the day before. He believed that Mrs Hodgson was somewhat out of control especially in so far as the "Voices" were able to swear and be generally rude without her admonishment since the excuse would be "The "Voice" made me do that"! In Billy's case it was interesting that he didn't stutter when he was swearing using the "Voice". He also thought that Mrs Hodgson was almost like the stage-manager of the show, but he felt sympathy for her difficult life. He did not put forward a conclusion as such, but found Janet to be "naughty, and observant, and bored, and a bit sad". He thought Margaret was "sadder", but going along with a "secret" which she was sharing with Janet.

Miss Mary Rose Barrington

Mary Rose Barrington attended on 13 January with John Stiles and Peter Hallson. She repeated a description of the situation on arrival already mentioned by Stiles (see above) and stated that "the only alleged phenomena that took place while we were there consisted of male voices talking disjointed obscenities while Margaret and Janet were in bed later that night". She, too, commented that the curtain twisting around Janet's throat could have been self-imposed even though Margaret confirmed Janet's denial of this. Barrington had perceptions to make about the differences between the girls' characters – Margaret more refined and Janet more "tomboyish and rather uncouth". She also upheld the sincerity of Mrs Hodgson and John Burcombe and found it "impossible to believe that they were deliberately deceiving" as they described the many happenings. Barrington's conclusion was that Mrs Hodgson was upset by the manifestations but "at the same time she obviously enjoys having interesting visitors". "... it is an entertainment in the life of the H. [Hodgson] family, and one they could never have enjoyed under normal circumstances".

Mr. Charles Moses

Charles Moses was the Vice President in Field Research of the Southern Californian Society for Psychical Research and his visit to Enfield was recorded at the time (24 January 1978). His ten-page report outlined the details of the people involved and the disturbances. He also compared the case with a case in Bridgeport, Connecticut in November 1974. He found Mrs Hodgson to be very tense which, he believed, may have influenced Janet as "the epicenter". He claimed that Margaret "... admitted helping or doing the 'Voice' but it would then get out of control. She further admitted that her throat would feel sore". In contradiction to Playfair's statement "Yet she never once coughed or even cleared her throat" there were several times on the tape collection as a whole where coughing by both girls could clearly be heard. Whether this was caused by the 'Voice' or natural causes is arguable.

His conclusions were varied. "I have the opinion that the sisters were responsible for the 'Voices'..." was one statement, but followed by "... poltergeist activity was most probably taking place" with its longevity being caused by all the attention it had received. He felt that the combination of Grosse being a compassionate father figure to the family combined with Mrs Hodgson's obvious loneliness were other contributory factors.

Dr Alan Gauld

Alan Gauld visited on the 12/13 November 1977. He brought with him various pieces of recording equipment, which he encouraged the girls to handle. No abnormal results were forthcoming and nothing happened during the night. [Gauld stayed overnight with Tony Cornell and Bernard Carr.] In the morning one of the water-filled balloons that Cornell had hidden under the bed in the children's room was thrown across the room and burst against the wall. Billy confirmed that he had seen this happen and Janet claimed that she had heard "the sound of scribbling coming from the floor…". "At 9:20 a.m. the second balloon went" and this led to water dripping through the ceiling downstairs. Cornell and Carr undertook further conversation with the family, which Gauld commented upon.

He concluded that, "Nothing occurred while we were in the house that the girls could not have perpetrated themselves". He wondered whether it was being staged for their benefit … "at times there was a good bit of laughter and high jinks". He, nevertheless, believed in Mrs Hodgson's "good faith" and praised John Burcombe's "very clear accounts".

Dr Ivor Grattan-Guinness and Mrs Grattan-Guinness

Ivor Grattan-Guinness wrote a brief account of his visit to the house "one evening in February" [1978]. He, in the company of his wife, believed that any previous psychic activity had now "been submerged under the publicity and general anxiety in the family". He was unable therefore to "find any evidence from this [his visit] conclusively in favour, or against, the veracity of their phenomena".

Mrs Grattan-Guinness' account was similarly brief. She commented on John Burcombe's seeming integrity, but found the girls' "deep chest voices" to be a "possible hysterical development". She continued: "The two girls obviously very much enjoyed the 'Voices', and one got the definite feeling of a show being put on for the benefit of the visitors."

Dr Carl Sargent

Carl Sargent sent a letter to the SPR (dated 10, July 1978) where he stated he would send a report later on. This was either not sent or it has not been found in the SPR archives. In his letter he made one significant assertion, which was that in the opinion of the Nottinghams, nothing paranormal had occurred "since the turn of the year". He asked for the information concerning his "third visit" to be confidential.

Mr. Lawrence Berger

Lawrence Berger visited the Enfield house on six occasions and kept notes for three visits in September, October and December 1977. During his visits he claimed "up to fifty ostensibly paranormal events took place, many of which I regarded as probably being genuine, but I was never in a position to be able to swear personally to their paranormality". He gave one example, which he believed came close to this:

> ... during the evening of 16/10/77. I was standing in the living room just by the entrance to the kitchen when Janet was coming out of the kitchen, there being nobody else in there. She was about one yard from me and facing me when there was a loud scraping noise from the kitchen behind her. I immediately pushed her aside to see what had happened and found the kitchen table had been twisted away from the wall. I do not think she could have done this without me seeing her.

He mentioned conversations with David Robertson and a technical expert from Pye, both of whom provided him with very credible and convincing accounts. He found the violent trances very disturbing and was concerned that suitable medical/psychiatric care "was not forthcoming".

Professor John Hasted

John Hasted visited the Hodgson household on 19 April 1978. [This date is a contradiction to what was specified on one of the recordings.] He described the people present [the family] and the fact that David Robertson was in attendance with "our video equipment" as well as Maurice Grosse and a *National Enquirer* photographer. He outlined the reports given by John Burcombe and the details of urine and excrement being found. Levitation was also spoken of and the "adults" played the levitation "game" – the children weren't interested. [I presume this was the party trick whereby a group of people lift a seated person into the air with just their fingertips.] After the adults went upstairs to set-up the video equipment, a bang was heard downstairs where Janet and Margaret were waiting to get ready for bed. Janet seemed unperturbed, but Margaret seemed genuinely scared – the light had blown and "swung violently" with damage to the lampshade and a chair had overturned. Hasted later examined the bulb and found the reason for its blowing "very unusual in my experience". Towards the end of his visit Hasted heard all three children's "Voices".

His assessment was "that there have been physical events of a 'poltergeist character' observed by various people in this house". His judgement of the "Voice" was that it was a case of "automatism" similar to "belly talking" and "characterized physiologically as originating in the false vocal chords".

Mr. Peter Dear

Peter Dear stayed overnight on 27/28 February and 18/19 March 1978 with Carl Sargent. He said that there were "no events which I would regard as paranormal" since they always occurred when they could not see the event and often when they were "out of sight of the children". He continued, "... the almost incessant 'Voice phenomenon' from Janet soon became tediously normal". And he was convinced it was the "product of Janet's own highly active mind" and imitated by Billy. He was generally damning about the source of the phenomena and reiterated, "The general feeling I got was that the family enjoyed the attention and the visitors they were getting". He mentioned the visitors' book, which was proudly presented, but was sensible enough to refuse to pronounce on the basis of two visits when he believed nothing paranormal happened. He concluded that the case may have started as genuine, but as it had progressed, by December for instance, it had entered the realm of children cheating when the phenomena were not forthcoming.

Mrs. Anita Gregory

Anita Gregory replied to the EPIC questionnaire directly, one point at a time. For reasons of space, I cannot reproduce her whole report, but in line with my desire not to reproduce vague impressions, I shall limit her replies accordingly:

- "I at no time personally witnessed any events that I would have been even tempted to regard as paranormal".
- "Mr. Carl Sargent has told me he obtained above-chance scores on RNG apparatus".
- "... I cannot quite believe that Mr. Grosse and Mr. Playfair did not witness some of the events they said they did. However, their readiness to

accept as paranormal quite easily explicable
happenings (in my view explicable that is)
inclines me to feel very reserved and cautious
about putting too much reliance on their faith
in the paranormality of what they witnessed".

Gregory was later awarded a Ph.D. from London Metropolitan University with the thesis 'Problems in investigating psychokinesis in special subjects' (1983) where she was particularly harsh on the legitimacy of the 'Enfield Poltergeist Case'. [A detailed opposition to her comments about the Enfield Poltergeist Case can be found in Engwer, 2017.]

Mr. George Fallows

George Fallows, who was a reporter at the beginning of the case, declined to make a "useful formal statement" since he did not witness anything unusual himself, although he was present when others claimed to do so. He stated that he had passed his notes to his colleague Bryan Rimmer at the time and that he had discarded them.

Mr. Douglas Bence

Douglas Bence, who was also a reporter at the time, did not wish to expand on the statements posed by the questionnaire since he was aware that the memory can play tricks. Instead he submitted a copy of the original article he published in *The Daily Mirror*. A "copy" attributed to Douglas Bence did not expand on anything that was either not already known or said before, apart from one contradiction, since the copied report stated that Vic [Nottingham] was hit on the back with a piece of Lego whereas his wife had reported earlier that he had been hit on the elbow with the Lego.

Dr Hugh Pincott

Hugh Pincott sent a long and detailed account of his various visits to Enfield and his opening remarks made it clear that whether things related were paranormal or not should be "left to subsequent judgement", however, he continued "they appeared to happen". Pincott's reports were presented according to his dates of visit and I shall follow accordingly, but, once again, only summarizing an outline of what he wrote.

5, December 1977

He arrived during the evening and met the family – Grosse and Robertson were already there. The past incidents were outlined. From memory he recalled Mrs Hodgson saying "Of course, we all used to think it was an evil spirit in the early days, but between you and me, I reckon it is to do with Janet's subconscious mind... It can be a bit of a nuisance sometimes, but I try my best to ignore it...". During this visit he pointed out a possible defect in one of Robertson's machines. Early the following morning the double bed had been moved allegedly by itself, but he did not witness this.

14, December 1977

He was brought up to date and told that the "Voice" had said earlier "I'll put on a fucking show for him". He reported that he was told to "fuck off" by the "Voice", but that Robertson seemed to have more luck, especially since the "Voice" wanted to talk about explicit sexual matters. When the subject turned to periods, Pincott was allowed into the room on the understanding that he would answer the questions which soon expanded into other sexual matters. Playfair required tighter tests and Janet's mouth was taped to see if she could still produce the "Voice" which Pincott recounted "... still continued with equal distinctness and clarity". He stayed the night but nothing else happened.

20. December 1977

He undertook this visit with Anita Gregory who "goaded the entity into alleged physical activity", but the eventual flying slipper was discounted by her as being physically thrown. Again an overnight stay produced no phenomena.

19, February 1978

He was joined by Eleanor O'Keeffe (SPR Secretary) and Francis Huxley. Most of the phenomena seemed to be falsified, but Margaret allegedly witnessed some movement in the toilet area, which Pincott investigated with mixed reactions.

His conclusion (labelled 'Personal Views') presented a brief history of how the case came about and its importance. He did not wish to comment about the case in too much detail but he did write:

This case will end up by being the best researched, best observed, and best documented or recorded effort this side of 1882, purely on account of the sheer volume of investigator hours invested and the academic attention mirrored upon it (for or against). Let me also say immediately, that I have every admiration for the way the investigators have conducted their affairs, irrespective, once again, as to how it may ultimately eventuate".

I have no views on Enfield except to say that phenomena recorded earlier on, seem more spontaneous than those noted later.

Mr. John Fuller

He replied via a letter about his and his wife Elizabeth's single visit to Enfield in early November 1977. He mentioned that Elizabeth "tried an informal reading" and acquired some accurate information that she hadn't previously known about. Nothing happened when they visited Enfield together and the children weren't there, but Fuller did take the opportunity in his letter to praise Playfair saying he was "...very clinical in his approach, and used great self-restraint in not jumping to conclusions".

Dr Bernard Carr

Bernard Carr sent his report to the SPR on 8, October 1978 and admitted to having to "report from memory" since his notes were in England and he was in America. He provided details of his visit (with Tony Cornell and Alan Gauld) and wrote that, "I cannot claim to have seen anything which convinced me of its paranormal origin". Various incidents did occur which were alleged, by others, to be paranormal. He thought he heard Billy refer to the investigators as "silly idiots", but admitted that his speech impediment made this difficult to verify.

In concluding, Carr felt that Mrs Hodgson and John Burcombe were both honest, but possibly gullible and he felt that Grosse and Playfair were, too. His assessment was that the phenomena were a mixture of genuine and fraudulent, but they had been sustained by the "children playing around" and that they had ceased by the time of his visit.

Miss Eleanor O'Keeffe

Having stressed her role as an observer and not an investigator, Eleanor O'Keeffe stated that she did not witness anything that impressed her "as of a psychic or mystical nature". She remarked that Janet's "guttural voice" could have been made by anyone as a childish prank and she saw that her lips were obviously moving. She also saw Billy move the chair he was sitting on and turn it over "a usual case of a young child trying to attract attention…" and she further felt that the family, "were enjoying some satisfaction in being the centre of attraction for so many experienced people, in fact, people they would not normally come in contact with". She concluded, "I can but hope that a factual statement by an uncommitted observer might find a place amongst numerous other reports by experts, and serve to lend balance".

Mr. Richard Grosse

Richard Grosse, the son of Maurice Grosse, delivered a very detailed report running to some eleven pages of script. He provided background details of the case leading to his own visit as well as a concise description of the house in Enfield and the people involved. He then went on to describe the events that he witnessed personally and especially the conversation with the "Voice" coming from Janet. Some of the time the "Voice" (which referred to itself as "Bill") spoke about matters of a "sexual nature" and Richard Grosse tried to change the conversation to one about religious matters, which was not productive. In his final observations he believed that there was no physical explanation for the "Voice" that Janet produced over an extended period of time. He mentioned that he felt Janet may have had "mind reading" capabilities because some of his thoughts were seemingly anticipated by her. Richard Grosse's final point was to stress the "honesty and integrity" of Mrs Hodgson and to state that "I consider that certain incidents that occurred the evening I visited the house are without normal or physical explanation".

Dr Peter Hallson

Peter Hallson visited the Hodgsons' house with Mary Rose Barrington and John Stiles on 13 January 1978 and he was brought up to date with the incidents that had occurred there. He believed that the curtain being wrapped around Janet's throat was instigated by her and that during his subsequent "five minutes or so" whilst he was in the room there was nothing to suggest anything from a "paranormal origin"... "rather the reverse". His conclusion was that events experienced by others should be treated with caution, but not ruled out.

General conclusions regarding the witnesses, investigators and phenomena and the committee members' own views.

Some of the conclusions and views reported were requested to be "confidential" and I shall uphold this principle. However, I shall present some of the information conveyed without necessarily naming the people involved. The full report of the committee is available at the SPR office in London.

The members of the committee were in agreement about several aspects of the case. They found John Burcombe to be "... an intelligent and careful observer" and that the Nottingham family were generally "fairly intelligent and sensible". The committee wrote of Grosse and Playfair, "We do not doubt their sincerity, and think that they have been scrupulous in reporting only what they believe themselves to have seen or heard". They might have added that the investigators also reported a vast amount of information that was conveyed by other witnesses. They disagreed with Grosse and Playfair concerning the origin of the "Voices" which they (the committee) thought were abnormal rather than paranormal.

One member of the committee highlighted the ripping out of the fireplace, which originally did not seem to have been tape-recorded, but scrutiny by the researcher Jason Engwer later suggested that the fireplace incident was "discernible on the tape" (private correspondence, December 2018). However, the text from the same committee member maintained:

> I personally rule out on grounds of sheer improbability that Janet or Margaret (or both), let alone Mrs. Harper (Hodgson) or Billy, deliberately ripped out the fireplace, while in a normal state of consciousness. Is it plausible to suppose that Janet, in a very much altered state of consciousness, not only acquires the capacity to speak in a bass growl, but also acquires the strength of ten, and in that state rips out the fireplace and hurls it across the room, endangering her brother's life?

Another member brought attention to the fact that the film *The Exorcist* was showing at cinemas "shortly before the Enfield troubles commenced" and that this may have influenced the way the alleged poltergeist developed. He thought that "possible mischief by the children [was] the most serious problem". However, another comment was "… that in the opening stages at least the case appeared to show paranormal aspects … i.e. not from currently known cause or conscious fraud".

CHAPTER THREE

The personal thoughts of Maurice Grosse

Introduction

Maurice Grosse was quite meticulous in putting his thoughts to paper as well as recording them in the audio collection. What is very apparent from the dialogues and scripts were his genuine concerns for the Hodgson family and a desire to help them during what proved to be a difficult time. However, this was combined with a wish to investigate to the best of his ability the possible paranormal origin of the phenomena, which he and others witnessed. In a typed archival report Grosse stated:

It has been particularly noticeable that Janet misses the authority and affection of a father, and at first she was very attached to Graham Morris. To some extent she has now turned her attentions to me. I have had to be very careful not to get too personally involved with the family and at the same time to give the personal attention that they so obviously require ... this sort of enquiry can only be conducted with the welfare of the family as the main consideration. This consideration has frequently inhibited the conduct of the enquiry" SPR Archives.

He was inexperienced as a psychical researcher, but his numerous patents for several successful inventions indicate that he nevertheless possessed a finely-tuned brain with all his mental and physical faculties in fine fettle. He enjoyed a full family life, which was only pained by the death of his daughter in a motorbike accident, and he participated fully in the Jewish community as well as still being involved in his business ventures. Perhaps a flaw in his investigational attitude was to adopt a 'paranormal' definition before completely eliminating all natural possibilities... understandable although this was at times when he was describing very unnatural activities in sometimes hysterical situations. He stated that "... an enormous amount of para-normal [sic] activity has taken place in 284 and to a lesser extent in 272 during the last two months". [Meaning September and October 1977 and '272' referring to the Burcombe family's house in Green Street.]

Reports

In a report dated 1 November 1977 Grosse reported that as early as 5 September 1977 "the poltergeist phenomena had all the appearances of being quite genuine". He felt the numerous witnesses were reliable and that "Janet is the epicentre" with most of the phenomena taking place "within a six feet radius" of her. During the time that she and the family were away on holiday, Grosse visited the house and reported that there was no active phenomenon.

In the same report Grosse suggested that some of the incidents were more suggestive "... of a 'haunting' rather than a poltergeist..." He listed the "brushing past a person and walking up the stairs" as well as "the laughing, crying, and moaning that have been heard, and the pulsating light seen at the top of the stairs".

He addressed the 'thorny' problem of the children "helping the phenomena along", maintaining that he would have been surprised if the children had not copied the phenomena. However, he insisted that it was "patently obvious" when the event was not genuine. Indeed he went further and stated, "I can safely say that at least 95% of the events that have taken place while I have been present have been genuine".

His report dated 23 April 1979 mentioned, "... while the family were having lunch in the kitchen, a considerable amount of P. K. activity took place". He referred to a washing up brush that flew at him "... from the direction of Margaret and Janet who were talking together at the time" and a little later on "... an apple flew across the kitchen from the direction of Janet and hit me on the shoulder." The settee moved when Johnnie was sitting next to it and when Grosse went to the toilet and was not present, "... two stones appeared in the living room and landed by the sideboard." He put these incidents down to P. K. (psycho-kinesis) activity. On returning home from this visit a further "strange happening" took place involving a car's engine running when there was no key in the ignition and it was securely locked. This arose outside his house and was witnessed by a neighbour from whom he went to the trouble to obtain a signed statement. On another occasion (30 March 1981) having just attended Johnny Hodgson's funeral, his car was seen by a neighbour to be leaking petrol in a manner which, he believed, was not possible.

Grosse's 'Some Thoughts on the Case' (SPR Archives) provides further insights. In the opening section he stated that he knew he had a "genuine case" on his hands, which would turn out to be "one of the most prolific of all time". He discarded what he described as "the Freudian explanation" that is the "exteriorization of the subconscious mind making itself apparent by actively effecting [sic] its physical surroundings". He made his feelings quite clear about the deliberations of experts:

> Sometimes the so-called experts' explanations for the activity would be more appropriate between the covers of *Alice in Wonderland*, for the statements they make are more intricate and complicated than the phenomena [sic] itself. (SPR Archives).

Grosse's attacks on sceptical scientists continued in an aggressive vein and culminated with "... it seems that the more positive the evidence that is produced for the existence of the 'inexplicable', the more likely the sceptic is to reject that evidence." He continued later on with

"...eminent scientists denying the existence of the paranormal are based on crass ignorance of the subject."

Although not strictly a report, but nevertheless a written statement, Grosse's lecture to the College of Psychic Studies in 1990 highlighted the intensity of his feelings about the Enfield occurrences and his contempt for the attitudes of some researchers and scientists. One of his less explosive comments was: "Our critics, who have a strong tendency to ignore the positive and accentuate the negative, are often shown respect from our own members that they do not deserve". He referred to the Committee for the Scientific Investigation of Claims of the Paranormal (CSICOP) as "jokers" who "destroy not only our evidence with their scurrilous and frequently ill-founded comments, but also our reputations."

Discussion

Maurice Grosse believed passionately in the veracity of the phenomena that he witnessed at Enfield and, at times, he was angered by the disbelief of those who disagreed with him, especially when they had not spent the many hours in attendance at the Hodgsons' home. Although he was inexperienced as a psychical investigator, his pragmatic attitude as an inventor was invaluable in cases where a considerable degree of common sense was necessary. His copious note-taking, multiple audio-recordings and instigation of diary-keeping by Mrs Hodgson are examples of this. He combined this with genuine care for the family, which was often commented upon even by his critics. His entry into psychical research may have been influenced by the death of his daughter, but whether this sad event had any influence upon his investigation of the Enfield Poltergeist Case, must be open to considerable question.

CHAPTER FOUR

Comparisons and Contrasts
between the 'Enfield Poltergeist
Case' and the 'Mount Rainier Case'

Introduction

I shall not repeat the details of the 'Enfield Poltergeist Case' since they have been covered throughout the script of this and many other books and documents. However, the so-called 'Mount Rainier Case' is less well-known and I shall, therefore, provide a rough outline as to what was claimed by the various commentators and, in some instances, those who allegedly witnessed the phenomena.

There are numerous published works on this subject and they are often contradictory and/or exaggerated.

One is often left with the adage "Who are you going to believe"? The case was further complicated by an array of different pseudonyms to protect the main characters in the action. Rosemary Ellen Guiley (1992) provides a concise explanation of the details of the case as it is generally portrayed. In January 1949 a child variously named as 'Roland' and 'Robbie' born 1, June, 1935, witnessed, together with his family, scratching sounds coming from the walls and ceiling of their house in Mount Rainier, a Maryland suburb of Washington D.C. (This address was disputed by Mark Opsasnick in *Strange Magazine*, claiming that the actual address was Cottage City, a short distance away.) The actual name of the boy was Douglas Deen, but he was nearly always referred to in the literature as 'Roland' or 'Robbie' and I shall follow suit by using 'Roland'. Pest control was not able to identify the problem and isolated 'squeaky' footsteps also started to be heard. Matters became worse when Roland's bed started shaking and objects such as dishes, fruit and furniture started moving of their own accord. His parents believed that a recently deceased aunt might be behind the disturbances since she used to use the Ouija board with Roland and they subsequently called upon their minister, Luther Miles Schulze for help. He did not favour a diabolical interpretation, being positively disposed towards parapsychology, but nevertheless he led prayers in church to try to dispel whatever was happening to the boy. The activity surrounding Roland worsened and, even when staying at the minister's own home, the bed vibrated and an armchair, in which he (Roland) was sitting, "scooted backward several inches" and finally "slammed into the wall". Throughout these incidents he appeared to be in a trance.

In February a new and worrying phenomenon arose when scratches started to appear on his body conveying messages. These included "Go to St Louis" which was where the fore-mentioned aunt had lived and his current cousins lived. The accounts concerning what happened next vary. Allen (1994) details an exorcism held at Georgetown University Hospital where the presiding clergyman was attacked, but other accounts omit this event. (Guiley, 1994) However, the family moved to St Louis on 5 March and the Roman Catholics, specifically Jesuits, were asked to perform a formal exorcism. Father William S. Bowdern, Raymond Bishop and Walter Halloran went through the rigorous processes to be given permission to undertake the ceremony. They took turns in leading the ritual, which was undertaken "no fewer than twenty times". During these sessions, numerous confrontations occurred. Roland thrashed and screamed; welts and scratches appeared on his body with increasing intensity; and furniture moved of its own accord. He could only be held down with great difficulty and he spat and kicked out continuously; attacked the priests in attendance; tried to bite them and urinated and passed wind frequently. In addition to this he allegedly barked like a dog; swore and used foul/sexually explicit language, emitted "diabolical" laughter and spoke in a "deep menacing voice that could not have come from a young boy" (Allen, 1994, p. 135). He also claimed that his throat and his penis were "on fire". The priests and his family decided that he should be baptized to try to drive the evil away. On the way to the ceremony he attacked the driver and there was almost a bad crash. It was commented (Allen) that during this incident the car radio burst into static [white noise?] even when it was turned off. Gradually the attacks subsided and, after Roland's return to Washington in April, they had disappeared altogether.

Schulze was in contact with J. B. Rhine, the director of the Parapsychology Laboratory at Duke University, but, in contrast to the exorcists' spirit possession theory, he believed that "... the phenomena were expressions of the boy's own unconscious ability to influence the objects in his environment and his own body through the power of his mind." (Guiley, 1994, p. 227)

Opsasnick (1999/2000) mentioned *The Parapsychology Bulletin*, August 1949, no. 14 containing an article 'The Truth Behind the Exorcist' and an in-depth article appeared in the January 1975 edition of *Fate* magazine, which provided further details (Erdmann, 1975). He undertook further detective work to try to uncover the truth behind the story, especially since a diary, that had not been made publically available, evidently gave specific details of what was generally quoted by some authors. He tracked down Father Halloran and put several questions to him, whose answers seemed to contradict what had been claimed elsewhere:

> Opasnick: "Did the boy speak in any language other than English?"
> Halloran: "Just Latin".
> Opasnick: "Did it appear he understood the Latin he was speaking?"
> Halloran: "I think he mimicked us"
> Opasnick: "Was there any change in the boy's voice?"
> Halloran: "Not really."
> Opasnick: "When the boy struck you in [sic] the nose, did he exhibit extraordinary strength?"

> Halloran: "I don't know. I never even thought very much about it. It certainly wasn't Tyson hitting me in the nose or something like that."

Further interviewing revealed that Halloran believed that the boy was not making the skin markings himself, but that it was hard to tell what the words were that actually appeared. Of course, it is possible that Father Halloran was recounting what the Church required him to or that, in the interim time, his memory had started to fade. Opsasnick concluded that there was a need for "close scrutiny" of the sources of information provided by the press and individual accounts. He believed that the boy's behaviour was in accordance with a youth who wanted to avoid a particular school via "throwing tantrums". When strapped to his bed he reacted strongly as might be expected and he was almost certainly in need of psychiatric help. His investigators "emphasized information that fitted their own agendas".

Comparing and contrasting the two cases.

Both cases started with noise phenomena that were witnessed by the families concerned and involved children as the focus for the activity. Both sets of phenomena increased in quantity and potency as the weeks/months progressed and were scrutinized by different investigators. There were many witnesses at different times, including neighbours, friends and other family members with different viewpoints. Movement of objects, seemingly by their own volition, was common and beyond the physical capabilities of the children; unknown footsteps were heard in both locations. Janet and Roland displayed violent physical activities, which damaged themselves and others around them during hysterical fits or whilst in trance. They were both thrown around and out of bed. They spoke in voices that were gruff and in a bass tone using language that was not normal in their daily routine – this included swearing, abusive and sexual language of a crude nature as well as screaming and laughing. Urine and other bodily functions were factors in both cases. The children both had a desire to sing popular songs that would have been known to them individually. With Janet and Roland, school attendance was an issue as neither of them wanted to attend their own specific schools and neither appeared to live in an academic environment. There were examples of automatic writing from both children and vivid dreams. They were certainly the focus of attention from numerous people once the phenomena started, which usually occurred during nighttime. Both children acted like any 'normal' children outside of their outbursts and psychiatrists were not particularly helpful in either case. Concerning the boy, one psychiatrist "declared that he did not believe the phenomena and he reported that he believed Robbie to be normal." (Allen, 1984, p. 11) Both children grew up to lead relatively normal lives and were seemingly unscarred by their traumatic times in childhood. If one was to dwell on just the similarities of the two cases then it might seem that there was a great deal in common; however, there were also some equally profound differences.

The gender of the two children was bound to have an effect on their subsequent behaviour. During their vocal outbursts Janet was very interested in girl-orientated themes (periods, menstruation etc.) whereas Roland talked about masturbation and his penis. Janet undoubtedly had a crush on the photographer Graham Morris and may have also 'fancied' some of the other younger men in attendance. Roland did not appear to have similar feelings for his investigators, who were admittedly mainly of the same sex. From the quoted sources it would appear that Janet was cruder and more persistent with her swearing than Roland, but perhaps this was because her episodes lasted a year or so, compared with just a few months in Roland's case. She was also involved with a greater range of objects moving than Roland, which included alleged teleportation through a wall of both herself and a book as well as her own levitation. The stone-throwing that was witnessed at Enfield did not occur according to the records during the 'Mount Rainier Case'. Janet did not suffer from the bleeding scratches, which Roland endured. The family set-ups were different as Roland was an only child and Janet had three siblings. He was a quiet individual who enjoyed 'Monopoly' whereas Janet was an active and proficient gymnast with an extrovert personality to match. When Janet was away from the family home – in hospital and on holiday – the activity almost totally ceased whereas Roland maintained his frenzies in other locations.

Almost certainly the biggest contrast between the two cases was concerning the nature of the investigators who attended the families. Although both cases involved members from religious organizations as well as the non-religious, the main focus of Roland's examination was from religious and specifically Jesuit sources, whereas the Hodgson family's case was undertaken by two psychical researchers, namely Maurice Grosse and Guy Playfair. The contrast between the people is shown below.

THE 'ENFIELD POLTERGEIST CASE'	THE 'MOUNT RAINIER CASE'
The investigators	**The investigators**
Maurice Grosse: Inventor, practicing Jew, psychical researcher	**Luther Miles Schulze**: Lutheran minister
Guy Playfair: Author, journalist, psychical researcher	**Father Raymond Bishop**: Jesuit priest
Others: Members of the Society for Psychical Research	**Father William Bowdern**: Jesuit pastor
Occasional mediums and psychics Members of the public	**Father Walter Halloran**: Jesuit scholastic
Occasional scientists, psychiatrists, psychologists, a hypnotist	**Others**: Jesuit priests and family members
Neighbours and family members	Occasional psychiatrists, psychologists

Although exorcism was more or less a last resort used by the Jesuits and undoubtedly in good faith, nevertheless their approach was very different from the methods used by Grosse and Playfair. The Jesuits' tools to combat the problem consisted of Roman Catholic ritual enhanced with holy water, candles, the cross and the Bible, whereas the psychical researchers used experimental procedures such as Raudive tests and attempts at communication via spiritualistic rapping. Mrs Hodgson was asked from the very start to keep a diary of events and, when possible, audio and photographic recordings were made. Janet undertook scientific testing under the supervision of the neuropsychiatrist Peter Fenwick at the Maudsley Hospital in London. Grosse was wary of mediums, but allowed people, suitably vetted by Playfair, to be invited into the house. Grosse genuinely seemed to feel a great amount of sympathy and compassion for the situation that the family was encountering, which may, at times, have clouded his judgement. That's not to say that he didn't get angry and frustrated when he believed that the children, and Janet in particular, was deceiving him. The variety of different people that attended Enfield produced a much broader outlook on what was happening, which should have been helpful and was... some of the time. The level of secrecy around the 'Mount Rainier Case' could not be applied to the 'Enfield Poltergeist case' where more people, both sceptics and believers, had an opportunity to witness what was happening.

So were they possessed?

Since I am neither a psychiatrist nor an exorcist I shall not pass an opinion one way or the other! Perhaps some evidence of what 'possession' might mean from a few sources will allow the reader, to make his/ her own mind up! Currently (December 2018) Google lists four hundred and ninety six million hits for the word 'possession'! Just how many of these are in any way learned or academic I dread to think. The folklorist and former president of the SPR held that:

> They (the possessed) speak in voices not their own, they act in a manner alien to their natural character, they are said to utter prophecies, and to display knowledge which they could not have normally acquired, and, in fact, do not consciously possess, in their normal condition (Lang, 1900, p. 129).

Canon Dominic Walker, an expert on religious exorcisms, stressed that commonsense and prayer would probably be more useful than "the rite of exorcism". He said, "I have to admit to being very skeptical about whether or not it is possible for someone to be possessed." (Underwood, 1990, p. 93) A major source of reference, and one that was used by Grosse and Playfair, during their investigation, was T. K. Oesterreich's *Possession: Demoniacal and Other* (1930). It provides a detailed look at the phenomena in a reasoned and reasonable manner, which is pertinent, in places, to the activities encountered in the two cases studied. Although he denies that the first appearance of possession is connected with any given time of life, which contradicts the "it all begins at puberty" idea, he insists the "predominance in women is extraordinarily marked (p. 121) and especially in the mildest cases when the uneducated are concerned. He reinforces both Charcot and Richer's writings in comparing the "contortions and violence of excitement" witnessed in hysterical states with alleged possession:

During this kind of attack the loss of consciousness is not complete. Some patients even remain fully conscious of their state, and at the end of the fit assert that during its course they were unable, for all their efforts, to master their agitation. When they succeeded in doing so for a few moments they only ended by bringing on a more violent fit soon afterwards. (P. Richer, *Etudes cliniques sur la grande hysterie*, Paris, 1885 p. 202. Cited in Oesterreich, 1930, p. 126)

As far as children are concerned he does maintain that "children scarcely ever retain consciousness in their compulsive state, but are immediately dominated by the phenomenon" (*Ibid.* p. 82). This was certainly the case with Roland and Janet whose individuality may have not yet been capable of resistance. It rings true again with his assertion that in the Middle Ages the possessor was often a demon or devil, but that in "modern times" it was more frequently a spirit of the dead except in "spiritual establishments". He continues "... but general opinion no longer takes sufficient account of him [the devil] to allow him to play an appreciable part in the empirical life" (p. 186). Thus one has Janet's spirit of the dead and Roland's devil in his surrounding circumstances, both accommodated. Oesterreich also mentions the obscene voices that "generally betray a coarse and filthy attitude" (p. 21). He cites frequent examples of voice change, which were such a notable feature in the cases that they are worthy of recounting here:

In particular the top register of the voice is displaced; the feminine voice is transformed into a bass one, for in all the cases of possession, which it has hitherto been my lot to know, the new individuality was a man. Thus in Kerner's M. B. case a little girl of eleven years suddenly gave utterance to "a deep bass voice", and later to another, but always with a timbre qualitatively different from the normal (Cited in *Ibid.* p. 20).

Owen cites Hereward Carrington (a mid-twentieth century distinguished S. P. R. member and researcher) concerning the link between puberty and poltergeist activity; writing in 1930 he wrote:

An energy seems to be radiated from the body … when the sexual energies are blossoming into maturity … it would almost seem as if these energies instead of taking the normal course … find this curious means of externalization (Cited in Owen, *M. M. M.* p. 2227).

Owen also draws on the work of Sigmund Freud and Josef Breuer's series of papers called *Studies in Hysteria* in which they sought a scientific theory for the origins of hysteria. They highlighted the need to "work off" emotional tension via physical activity that might be "automatic and instinctive".

There is some reason to believe that it happens by an unconscious process, because the poltergeist person usually seems to have no control over the happenings and only the dimmest awareness that she or he is responsible for the happenings. (*Ibid.* p. 2228)

More recently, Terry Wright (1994) has brought the discussion about demonic possession up-to-date with:

"Few issues create as much friction between science and religion as demonic possession. Psychiatrists and priests are fiercely divided over the interpretation of cases in which a person appears to be possessed by another personality." (p. 175)

He summarises that a 'supernature' viewpoint might argue that, "in some rare cases of possession there really are paranormal phenomena (Wright, p. 199):

... possession can be both mental illness and spirit possession, each contributing to the other. The paranormal phenomena may be real and can be a product of a disturbed mind or an attribute of spirit. It might be argued that extra-sensory perception (telepathy) and psychokinesis are the only ways in which any spirit can interact with the physical world ... possession can be a manifestation of a reality beyond that described by science (p. 199-200).

Playfair endorsed this viewpoint several times during the Enfield investigation when he quoted Allan Kardec's doctrine of Spiritism with its 'subsystems' of past lives, popular in Brazil where he (Playfair) had lived in the past. An SPR founding father F. W. H. Myers devoted a whole chapter to the subject of possession in his two-volume magnum opus *Human Personality and its Survival of Bodily Death* where he stated that in possession "... the automatist's own personality does for the time altogether disappear, while there is a more or less complete *substitution* [Myers' italics] of personality;

writing or speech being given by a spirit through the entranced organism." (p. 189) With the possible addition of other words than just 'spirit', for instance, 'entity' or even 'schizotypy characteristics', Myers' definition seems still to provide a reasonable explanation of the state. Peter Underwood posed an interesting quandary in quoting Sir Leslie Shane (an Irish diplomat and author) who asked "But do the dead know they are haunting the living?" (Underwood, 1990, p. 37).

CHAPTER FIVE

Forty years on

Unfortunately, many of the original witnesses in the Enfield Poltergeist Case have died in the interim years and, most notably, Maurice Grosse and Guy Lyon Playfair. The Hodgson family similarly suffered the loss of Mrs Hodgson and her son Johnny. Several of the researchers who witnessed the Enfield phenomena have also died since then including John Stiles, Milbourne Christopher and Carl Sargent. However, I felt it would be of interest to the reader to learn whether the views of several key people had changed during the last forty years since the events occurred. Therefore, I set about contacting as many of these people as possible to give them a chance, if they wished, to express their views about the case in this publication. These opinions were very much their own and should not be interpreted as being either condemned or condoned by myself.

I prepared a letter to be sent, either electronically or via the standard postal system, to people at addresses where I hoped they might be living. I wanted to avoid any compulsion to reply and hopefully made this clear in the letter below:

Dear XXX

I am contacting you to enquire whether you would be willing to put into print a few words about your experiences at Enfield during the alleged poltergeist outbreak there between 1977 and 1978. If you would like to share any of these experiences I would be happy to have them printed in a forthcoming publication which seeks to express what happened at this time particularly via the audio-cassette tapes that I have transcribed and digitalized during the last few months. I do not intend to promote the case for or against the paranormalilty of the phenomena, but simply to describe what happened and let others interpret the information accordingly. Anything that you wrote would be acknowledged and your identity would be concealed if so desired. I would ask that your comments were not libellous or unlawful in any way to avoid editorial censorship.

If you would like to voice your opinion then kindly contact me and I shall respond in due course. Unfortunately I cannot offer any financial incentive for your participation.

YOURS SINCERELY, MELVYN J. WILLIN

I attempted to contact the appropriate people and was very pleased with the prompt reply from some of the contactees, notably Hugh Pincott, Alan Gauld, Mary Rose Barrington, David Robertson and Bernard Carr. Gauld, sent me a detailed report of his visit from his own un-published notes made at the time as well as a consideration of the phenomena based on his conversations with many people involved with the case both during and since its completion. Mrs Rainbow – the wife of John Rainbow a local tradesman who had witnessed Janet levitating – replied that unfortunately her husband had died in July 2018, but she confirmed that he had continued to believe that what he had seen was a genuine levitation. She added, "… he also had a witness who also saw what was happening." David Robertson's memories were particularly valued since he was a frequent visitor to Enfield and knew the family, friends and investigators well. Graham Morris telephoned me and we had a fairly long conversation wherein he gave me permission to quote him.

Despite my best efforts I was not able to find current contact details for the Burcombe family, Billy and Margaret Hodgson, Carolyn Heeps, Charles Moses and Dono Gmelig-Meyling. I contacted Janet Hodgson, the Nottingham family, Hazel Short, Matthew Manning and Peter Fenwick, but did not receive replies from them.

Printed below are the responses I received in reply to my letter.

Bernard Carr

I visited Enfield with Tony Cornell and Alan Gauld on the evening of 12 November 1977 and stayed overnight. Alan has already provided a description of that visit in this volume and my own impressions were recorded in a report I wrote in October 1978, as summarised in Chapter 3. However, I will take this opportunity to add some further reflections. I also co-organised the SPR conference in Cambridge in 1978, at which the presentation by Grosse and Playfair about the case attracted considerable controversy.

What I did not record in my report – since it was a purely personal matter – is that my visit to Enfield got me into trouble with my girlfriend at the time. This is because I was supposed to be co-hosting a party with her that evening but opted to stay at Enfield instead. I reasoned that there would be many opportunities to host parties but that this could be a once-in-a–lifetime opportunity to witness a good poltergeist case. However, I don't think my girlfriend was impressed with this argument. Nor did the visit endear myself, Alan and Tony to Playfair, since his book refers to our involvement in rather uncomplimentary terms.

As regards the "balloon-filled-with-water" incident, it should be emphasised that the balloon had been under the bed all night but only burst after the children were informed of this by Tony in the morning. The fact that the balloon had escaped the attention of the "spirit" rather bolstered my view that the children were responsible. When Tony rapped on the wall from next door in the morning, Margaret immediately inferred that it was "that man" (i.e. Tony). This was correct but it struck me as strange that she should immediately come to that conclusion if she believed that similar raps were generated by the poltergeist.

My claim – mentioned in Alan's account - that I overheard Billy referring to the investigators as "silly idiots who would believe anything" is clearly significant and certainly strengthened my impression at the time that the children were taking us all for a ride. However, after 40 years I no longer recall the remark itself (just my giving an account it) and also Billy had a speech impediment, so I'm not 100% confident about this.

Whatever the status of these three incidents, my opinion at the time was that, while the case may have been triggered by genuine phenomena, it was sustained by the children playing around. However, I was not an experienced investigator and I now regard that assessment as rather pretentious, especially since I was only there for one night. Certainly one remark in my report - "I would not be surprised to learn that all genuine phenomena had already ceased by the time I visited" – was questionable since the phenomena continued for another year.

Later I got to know both Grosse and Playfair much better – indeed they became friends - and I now hold a more positive view of their status as investigators. It's true that Grosse had little experience at the start of the Enfield case but he had a huge amount by the end and there is no doubting his sincerity and compassion for the family. After 40 years - just as with Scole case, which I also visited - I'm not sure what to conclude. For me personally perhaps the strongest reason to believe in poltergeists is that my good friend Tony Cornell spent a lifetime investigating them and came to conclude that some of them were genuine. Tony was rather sceptical of the Enfield case itself but– like me - he only spent one night there.

Hugh Pincott

As we know, Maurice Grosse was a latecomer to the SPR on account of his daughter being involved in a fatal motorbike accident. Like so many, he was extremely impatient with the lack of progress made by the SPR's research, and used every opportunity at general meetings or with officers to quote from and emphasise Sidgwick's Presidential Address in July, 1882:

> ... it is a scandal that the dispute as to the reality of these phenomena should still be going on, that so many competent witnesses should have declared their belief in them, that so many others should be profoundly interested in having the question determined, and yet that the educated world, as a body, should still be simply in the attitude of incredibility (*Proceedings of the Society for Psychical Research.* Vol. 1.).

We explained to him that opportunities for investigation did not arrive every day, and that we would contact him immediately something suitable came up. Still, he persisted.

While I was Honorary Secretary my work office was in Piccadilly, quite a short Number 9 bus ride from the Adam & Eve premises, so, usually twice a week, I spent a long lunch hour with the Secretary Eleanor O'Keeffe, transacting Society administrative business. On 1 September 1977, the telephone rang. *The Daily Mirror*: a poltergeist in Enfield; could we send someone to investigate? Nothing remarkable so far; the SPR received such calls regularly, occasionally several in a week. Eleanor promised to phone them back. Who could we recommend? Our most experienced member with poltergeists was Brian Nisbet at Croydon. A long way from Enfield, and he had been ill recently. Then I had an idea: 'Let's send Maurice Grosse: that will get him off our back for a bit!". Eleanor smiled broadly as she dialled the Mirror's number. Hardly had they answered before a gleaming red E-type Jaguar drew up outside a house in Enfield.

A week later, on the eighth, I was chairing a Society lecture – on *Poltergeists and Allied Phenomena* – given by new Librarian, Nick Clark-Lowes. During question time Maurice Grosse rose and announced: "I can tell you about poltergeists!" and proceeded to astound the audience. "But I need a lot of help now" he pleaded. First to approach him afterwards was Guy Playfair. ... Maurice attended a "new members' meeting" on 7 November, at which he played extracts from his growing volume of recording tapes – incredible sounds of purported poltergeist material. Once I had assigned a case to a member, my policy was not to interfere unless invited to do so. My invitation to Enfield on Monday, 5 December was trailed by Maurice reporting that the "entity" seemed to be developing a personality.

On arrival I was most impressed by the calm, unruffled attitude of Mrs Hodgson, a lovely uncomplicated Cockney lady. As she poured me a cup of tea in the kitchen she commented: "Of course, we used to think it was them evil spirits, but now it is more probably due to Janet's unconscious mind exteriorising her innermost fears and fantasies ..." "Yer wha'?!" I often quote this at training days as an excellent example of putting subjects at ease and offering possible explanations. Amid later controversies, not much credit has accrued to Guy and Maurice for achieving this. Meanwhile upstairs it was a fairly quiet night: I slept on the sofa below. Rising at 07:30 a.m. I heard a loud "thump" above and swift investigation showed a large bed on its side.

Maurice phoned me again in some excitement on 13 December: "The poltergeist now talks and materialises"! As I arrived for an observation the following evening a monitoring system was being set up. The "talking poltergeist" had improved its diction, now asking and answering questions. David Robertson and I were allowed to enter the girls' bedroom, but we were instructed by Janet to sit at the foot of the bed facing forward. She was tucked up securely with the edge of the top blanket positioned just beneath her nose, covering her mouth. Consequently, we could not identify where the deep, rough and very fluent voice was coming from: Janet or from some other entity? It was at this point that the Voice ("Bill") asked the famous question: "Why do girls have fucking periods?"

Shortly afterwards I proposed an experiment which has never been reported or published. I believed it would determine conclusively (so I thought) whether the Voice emanated from Janet or not. Simply fill her mouth with a coloured liquid, tape it closed and see what happens. Maurice felt Mrs Hodgson would not allow this: I asked her and she had no objection at all. So Janet willingly filled her mouth completely with cold tea, and we taped it closed securely. But ... the Voice continued to speak with undiminished clarity! By this stage, several of us for whom the spiritistic hypothesis was not a first choice, hunched our shoulders and looked around warily! And on removing the tape, Janet spat out a complete mouthful of tea. Of course this experiment served to confirm the later revelation of the laryngoscope examination by a colleague of Professor

Hasted that it was not the usual voicebox and resonating cavity producing the voices.

When David Robertson and I were sitting at the foot of the bed, the entity would quite happily throw items around on request. Cushions would be projected over our heads with some momentum, and, when we spun around within a fraction of a second, Janet was still tucked firmly in bed with no hint of bedclothes movement. One pillow passed through a curtained window ending up on the lawn below. I think Janet may secretly have fancied David, which might account for "Bill's" ready compliance. I left for work too early in the morning and failed to witness reported materialisations, disappearances and the pillow on the roof! On 20 December I visited Enfield again, with Anita Gregory, who had a pillow thrown at her, and we both witnessed the curtains moving unaided. This was probably the zenith for "genuine" phenomena, though a tail of well-attested events did extend into the following year.

After Christmas, several of the SPR's "big names" visited the house, but were distinctly unimpressed. By this time the three youngsters were mimicking the voice without even attempting to close their mouths. This and Mrs Hodgson's Visitors Book reinforced sceptical opinion in most visitors around this time. The sequel erupted (not too strong a word) at the "International" Conference in Trinity College, Cambridge on Wednesday, 29 March 1978. Maurice and Guy divided the allotted time between themselves and presented audio-visual material in a scientific, subdued, understated and unemotional way. I was shocked at the reaction when prominent academics during the discussion evoked savage controversy and unbelievable hostility. Why? Alas, at the time, there was a conviction among some senior members that only academics were capable of competent investigation (and that they alone should govern the Society): clearly Guy and Maurice were "trade". Furthermore there was an unfortunate tendency for some members to refuse cases because "I am too busy now, but will take it over when it gets interesting".

My verdict? The wealth of personal testimony indicates (up until Christmas, anyway) a huge incidence of happenings that defy everyday commonsense (i.e. highly paranormal). This is one of the classic cases – if only because of the sheer volume of recorded high-quality evidence – which should repay careful detailed study by future researchers.

Mary Rose Barrington

I remember being convinced by Mrs Hodgson showing me (there were just the two of us in the small back bedroom) how, when she made to leave the room, the chest of drawers moved out from the wall as if to obstruct her exit. I didn't think she had the imagination to think up something so weird but consistent with poltergeist phenomena. I was also favourably impressed by John Burcombe, Mrs Hodgson's brother, who described how his chair seemed to try to unseat him. I had no doubts about Maurice Grosse's description of how the kettle started dancing around on the top of the cooker while he watched it, and was the only person in the kitchen.

I have no doubt that physical phenomena occurred at Enfield, but, at the time, Maurice lay a lot of emphasis on the sporadic growlings of Janet in an allegedly trance state. This may have put a lot of people off Enfield. It was much later that she is said to have brought communications from a previous occupier, after the case had received a lot of publicity. I am impressed that Margaret and Janet have resisted blandishments to state that all the phenomena were their doing.

Alan Gauld

I must begin by saying that I was only marginally involved in the Enfield case. Fairly early in the case I paid one overnight visit to the scene of activities and subsequently reviewed the first edition of Guy Playfair's *This House is Haunted* (1980) for a psychology publication called *Psychology News* (now I believe defunct or transmuted. I have, however, drawn on parts of the review in the later parts of this article – I should remark that I sent copies to both Guy Playfair and Maurice Grosse and received no comments or complaints from them). I heard, however, a fair amount about the case from other SPR members who had become involved in it, and, later, I watched parts of various television programs (mostly very bad) centring on it.

My own visit to the house (on 12/13 November, 1977) descended at times into farce or something very near it. Guy Playfair had asked me, on the preceding day, to come and to bring with me whatever possibly useful pieces of scientific apparatus I could lay hands on (which at this short notice involved borrowing a few odds and ends that my neighbour, a physicist, happened to have in his house). Guy also gave me instructions as to finding the house and emphasized that I was to keep this information to myself. When I arrived, latish in the evening, I found, in addition to Guy Playfair and Maurice Grosse, two other members of the SPR, Tony Cornell and Bernard Carr, already present. The atmosphere was decidedly chilly, particularly in the neighbourhood of Guy Playfair. Afterwards (too late) I discovered that he thought I must have given the secret address away to Tony and Bernard, which I had not (they had simply got it from SPR Headquarters). Guy's suspicions not unnaturally fell on me, as a known associate of Tony and Bernard (I hasten to say that he and I later became quite friendly). It was, however, not an auspicious beginning to my visit.

Still, I was able to meet the three children (Margaret, 13, Janet, 11 and Billy, 7) and to talk with their mother and a neighbour, from both of whom, and from Maurice Grosse (a recently joined SPR member and first investigator of the case) I heard some straightforward and interesting accounts of things they had themselves witnessed. All this was very useful.

About ten o'clock the three children went to bed upstairs in the same bedroom. Soon afterwards the onset of allegedly paranormal happenings was heralded by thumps and excited squeals from upstairs, followed by noises as of mattresses being bounced upon as the girls were purportedly thrown out of bed or transported from one bed to another (phenomena which had been said to occur). Maurice Grosse, Bernard and I (joined later by Tony) went upstairs and stood outside the bedroom door (we had been informed that these events only happened when the children were alone in the room). Bursts of such sounds occurred regularly over about the next hour and a half, and often when the sounds indicated that something of interest might be imminent or taking place, Maurice would rush into the bedroom, hoping to catch the phenomenon in progress

(I cannot remember whether he had a camera in his hand) but although his energy and persistence were admirable, he had no luck. The girls, most notably Janet, round whom events seemed especially to centre, told us what had supposedly happened, which often included pillows being pulled out and thrown round. Tony and I were both of the opinion that for whatever reason Margaret was at times not entirely happy with Janet.

Tony and I also tried out some small magnetic compasses, a gold-leaf electroscope and an infrared detector, which I had borrowed (see above) to see whether the girls would be able to affect them other than through ordinary physical vibrations, but they were not. Tony further tried lying down on the double bed with the two girls but regrettably it neither moved nor pitched him off.

Eventually, as midnight got nearer, the children quietened down and subsided into sleep. Guy had already gone home. Tired from my long journey, not to mention the subsequent events, and being by that time quite convinced that no worthwhile evidence would be forthcoming that night, I went downstairs and tried to get what sleep I could on a chair in the living room. Bernard went to sleep in the spare bedroom, and Tony prowled around for some hours affixing telltale pieces of dark cotton in key places of which he gives a full list in his own account. He also rather rashly filled two balloons with water, placed them in separate saucepans from the kitchen, and, creeping in to the sleeping children's bedroom, pushed each under a different bed as bait for spooks or children.

After eight o'clock in the morning, the phenomena in the bedroom began again, so much so that Tony formed the opinion that the children did not want us to leave (which we were showing signs of doing). Meanwhile Bernard, standing quietly outside the bedroom door, overheard (as he told us) young Billy say, "These silly twits [the investigators] would believe anything." But the children had not yet discovered the hidden water-filled balloons. Tony pointed these out to them, and (I follow his own account here) remarked that their non-discovery did not reflect well on the psychic endowments of the spirits involved. Not long afterwards he left the room and the inevitable shortly happened. The floor and wall of the bedroom were copiously splashed. Hearing noises, I went upstairs to find out what had was going on, and returned downstairs with perhaps no very appreciative feelings about Tony's stratagem. Before long I discovered that water was coming through the ceiling boards in the living room. (I afterwards gathered this was from the second balloon). A lot of it was dripping down onto a birdcage with one small inmate. I moved the cage to one side and hoped the little budgie would not catch cold. 'Farce' is surely the right word for these events, but one could not altogether blame the children.

A final phenomenon took place at about half-past nine. I was with Margaret sitting in the living room and Janet and her mother were in the kitchen. Hearing a loud sound from the kitchen I looked up sharply and saw through the door that the kitchen table had been turned over. Janet was beside it, looking towards me with a curious expression, not as though she had not been alarmed by the sudden bang of the table but more as though she wondered what I might have seen.

In short, during our visit we had witnessed nothing that was incompatible with the obvious hypothesis of mischief by the children and quite a lot that suggested it. But to be fair neither had we seen anything that directly indicated it.

Before we left, Tony, who had been convinced from early on that the two girls were responsible for all the phenomena, gave them both a lecture, pointing out to them how stressful their antics must be for their mother (who was present). They said little but appeared to agree, as did Mrs H[odgson]. That was the end of my visit.

Tony later wrote from his notes a long and valuable account of his visit, and of his then and subsequent views on the case, which has never been published. It was eventually included as a couple of chapters in his book, *Investigating the Paranormal* (2002), but was excised by the publisher for fear of possible legal repercussions, probably unnecessarily, but there were also other times in the case when hints of litigation seemed to hang over it. The report of the SPR committee on the case was never published.

But to go back: The Grosse-Playfair investigation continued apace after our visit, and further SPR members and others visited the Enfield house. In March 1978 the two of them gave an account of the case at an international conference organized by the SPR. Their reception seems to have been somewhat hostile. Certain members of the audience were, Maurice and Guy felt, pedantically obsessed with the possibility of fraud, a possibility which they had ruled out to their satisfaction at an early stage as a *general* explanation of the happenings. The resultant disputes outlasted the conference for months, or indeed years, and became, at times, somewhat acrimonious as people, both within and outside the SPR, took sides. The leader of the SPR critics was the late Anita Gregory whose underlying feeling was clearly that the evidence in the case fell, on the whole, below SPR standards and that too much association with it might damage the Society's reputation. She reviewed *This House is Haunted* in the SPR Journal for 1980 and was involved in quite a few subsequent exchanges about the case. Some of her younger supporters developed a nice line in imitating the odd sounds and gruff voices which the girls had begun to produce under the influence of the supposed spirits. A paper embodying her final thoughts on the case still remains unpublished in the SPR Archives.

I was not involved in any of this, but, after the publication of Playfair's 1980 book, I could and still can sympathize with both sides. It seemed to me that a (rather limited) number of the reported events in the case, including some witnessed by the investigators themselves, were not readily susceptible of any normal explanation, and that Grosse and Playfair's annoyance at the merely armchair scepticism of their critics was, from their point of view, quite understandable. On the other hand, in his book, Playfair did not deal satisfactorily with the issue of fraud, which he mentions in passing several times, but immediately shies away from. He offers such remarks as: "We both knew that children involved in poltergeist cases often tended to imitate the phenomena, and although we eventually had definite proof that some of the H[odgson] children did this, it did not worry us in the least. Children learn everything by imitation, but this does not make what they imitate any less genuine." (Pp. 168-9.) That is all very well, but readers are surely entitled to be given full details of the fraudulent incidents in order to form their own opinions about what the children may have been up to. Such details constitute part of the essential background information in the light of which the case as a whole has to be assessed.

Furthermore, for many of the alleged phenomena we do not have the testimony of persons outside the family, and even when we do have such testimony, it is not always obvious that fraudulent manipulations were excluded. Playfair often seems to work on the implicit principle that because *some* phenomena, for which ordinary explanations were difficult to devise, took place before outside witnesses, most of the remaining phenomena are likely to have been genuine too. But it might reasonably be remarked that the children, who had probably never before had so much attention and excitement, had every reason to keep the pot on the boil. To visitors such as myself they often seemed to be pulling our legs, and who am I to blame them? In later years they have admitted to indulging themselves in this way, but have continued to deny that it was always so. Under these circumstances how can one properly evaluate what was going on unless one is given full details of the tricks that the girls are known to have played?

Doubting Thomases will not have found their doubts assuaged by Playfair's manner of presenting his material. If academic writers sometimes make no concessions to the general reader, Playfair made none to the academics. We find such sentences as "As soon as he received the call from the SPR, Grosse left his office . . . and within an hour . . . his gleaming red Jaguar was pulling up outside the H[odgsons'] house." A good deal of space is consumed with accounts of the author's thoughts and feelings as the case progressed, and much of the narrative proceeds through detailed reports (surely not taken down verbatim at the time) of conversations between various participants. Original notes, witnesses' original signed statements, logs of events, technical data from recording instruments

– in short all the hallmarks scientific or would-be scientific parapsychology – are very sparsely represented. It would be absurd to criticise Guy Playfair too strongly on these grounds (he makes it clear that his account is based upon extensive notes and recordings, and no professional writer can afford to be dull), but I cannot help feeling that the book might have been a good deal more impressive (and not just to academic readers) if he had added a few dozen pages (won perhaps by throwing out some of the reported conversation) in order to set forth samples of the original notes, statements, recordings, etc., on which his account is based. (From this point of view the supplementary article published by Playfair and Grosse in 1988 is rather nearer the mark – GLP and MG, Enfield revisited: The evaporation of positive evidence/ JSPR, 55, 1988, 209-19) Any person seriously interested in this or other debatable area would certainly wish to see, and is again entitled to see, specimens of such original sources so that he may assess what the author has made of them. It could be that the present volume will help to supply some of these missing requirements in the Enfield case and to clarify how we should regard the phenomena concerned.

David Robertson

In 1977 Maurice Grosse was investigating events at Enfield and, as things were getting difficult to cope with, he approached for advice Professor John Hasted from Birkbeck College, London University. He did this because by that time Hasted had accumulated a lot of experience working with paranormal metal bending effects and his work was known at the Society for Psychical Research. The SPR had also passed on the name and address of the Hodgson family to Maurice some time before.

I was helping with Hasted's paranormal work at Birkbeck as I considered these phenomena to be of importance to scientific knowledge. He had worked out how to facilitate metal bending effects and I was, by then, familiar with what he was doing even if I hadn't abstracted it into a detailed methodology. It was effective and most sessions produced many paranormal effects including bending, fractures, softening and sometimes teleportation. I was working on the electronics, building new detectors and testing them in various situations. We had independent sensors, laser pointer and strain gauge, later piezoelectric, capacitive and phase sensitive conduction detectors, and various control monitors to pick up interference, monitor and introduce body voltages.

On this occasion Hasted asked me to come into the meeting with Maurice, he knew that I had more time available and would be able to help with the case and, thus, reduce the pressure on the current investigators. The plan was for Maurice then to have regular meetings with Professor Hasted and discuss any difficulties and developments. I met Guy Playfair later at the house; he was quieter, had much previous experience of poltergeists, and was sharing the workload with Maurice. At the meeting, Maurice had with him a number of photographs taken by Graham Morris, showing Janet being thrown out of bed and Lego bricks flying. He also played some tapes and discussed the family breakup when the father left the house; the upset caused and the current problems with furniture being thrown around;

disruptions to the family routine and the general background. It was agreed that I should go to the house and be introduced to the family. Thereafter, if they were willing, I could watch what was going on and help with minimising the disturbances at bedtime. Hasted didn't have time to visit the house regularly himself but thought it important to have more people around, especially as I worked with him often and the families he was visiting to do metal bending experiments. In his experience the interactions between the experimenters and the family were sensitive to who was present. Hasted and his ancestors had a strong background with interpersonal skills, as I found out later when I read his memoirs.

During the first few days of visiting, I arrived in the afternoon and found that things were generally quiet with Mrs Hodgson welcoming the extra help. She had a very practical nature, usually working at home doing her housekeeping tasks. More events and disturbance tended to start once the girls, Janet and Margaret, got home from school. Billy was often in the house and, although young, was a very quiet boy who played by himself and watched what was going on around him.

I remember one time after the girls got home, Mrs Hodgson was doing some washing up in the kitchen and a packet of soap powder came out of the end floor level cupboard and scattered all over the floor. Everyone else was in the main room and otherwise busy, but they came in to help clean it up. The girls would often say that the poltergeist had pulled or thrown one or more of their school items while they were in the main room doing their homework. At first things usually, but not always, happened more while I was in another room or looking the other way. They said that this

134

type of annoyance had been going on for some time. In the evening between 6:00 p.m. and 8:00 p.m. Maurice or Guy would arrive. They took it in turns to help at the house, and I think that at weekends they were often both there so I could have a break. The family were all sleeping in the front bedroom by this time because the disturbances were too great if they split up. The problem at that point was that they would get pulled out of bed; have their hair pulled; objects would fly about and curtains and soft toys would move. It usually didn't prevent them sleeping in the end, but often meant that they got a short sleep and were tired in the morning. It was suggested that I could stay in the back bedroom, as trains to get home weren't available all night. I wasn't disturbed in the back bedroom and could sleep late enough to be well rested for the next day. Having someone in the house for emergencies was a comfort to the family.

I do remember one occasion when everyone was downstairs that Guy asked me to check the bedrooms as he thought he had heard a noise. I went up to have a look around, checked the back and front bedrooms, and then there was a huge crash from the back bedroom. Guy came running up the stairs and asked what had happened and where I was. I told him that I was on the landing by the stairs as it happened. We went into the back bedroom and one of the sets of drawers had been thrown right across the room onto its front. Guy was obviously asking himself if I could have thrown it, but, as I told him, I wasn't even in the room at the time. A cupboard like that would have been difficult for one person to move, in any case. I was aware that such forces could potentially be dangerous, but the main thing in my mind at the time was that it was interesting to see such large forces at work. Although this was undoubtedly paranormal it still didn't stop the effects often from manifesting while I was looking the other way. The presence of other people seemed to modify what happened. I was familiar with this from our work with other families and Hasted would often use this idea of having one or more people leave the room.

An example of this 'looking away' effect happened as I was going into the kitchen from the main room. As I reached the door, a shelf unit hurled itself front first onto the floor on my left. Janet was still sitting some way back in the main room. There were many smaller events disturbing the household too – plugs would be pulled out of sockets and items thrown off shelves onto the floor. I would tape the plugs into the sockets and collect up loose items. I took it too far one time with quite a big pile of items and, in the end, I had a heavy glass ashtray plate thrown at my head. Also, having a lot of red and black insulating tape in the bin meant that the poltergeist had the opportunity to use it to write messages on the bathroom door. There were also phenomena in the toilet, much to the embarrassment of the girls. I ignored this and usually tried to observe things without encouragement or criticism.

Over time I saw more things. There seemed to be two types of event: many disturbances occurred when I was not directly looking at what happened or when the forces acted on a person. There were also occasions when objects moved by themselves in full view. For example, candle holders sliding along a shelf without anyone being nearby or a curtain constantly moving without anyone touching it. When this happened the poltergeist clearly didn't care about our seeing what was going on and the phenomena, once started like that, would often continue for some time. On other occasions it would apparently do things to frustrate our observations and disrupt the family activities.

Maurice was very good at communicating with the poltergeist: by using knocks, he could create space for some story to develop. Over time the knocks evolved into grunts and a voice that could answer questions. It would usually swear and have little of value to say, but the method was useful for asking it to do things and it would often comply if you did what it asked, usually by leaving the room, but with family members generally being allowed to stay. This seemed to be a reasonable compromise.

I remember one occasion when I was communicating with the voice like this with Janet on the far side of the front bedroom and much earlier throwing of objects, voice phenomena and knocking. I came back into the front bedroom to ask Janet a few things and was by the bedroom door looking for something that had been last seen there. Loud knocks started coming from the bed board next to my head. Janet was the only other person in the room and she was over near the far corner on her bed by the window. The knocks kept on for some time and I commented to her about it. This is somewhat unnerving with clearly loud paranormal knocks right next to my head that went on for some time. I wasn't sure what to do and started to write down what was happening to distract myself from thinking about it too much. Maurice had the skill of attributing it to an intelligent entity and communicating with it. I was used to the voice phenomena and so didn't try to communicate separately with the knocks, but I think the process of working at a higher level of abstraction is a good one since it takes the mind off distractions like the paranormal nature of things and can also be used to build things up and use energy in a benign way, at least benign internally to the family. It is often done with Ouija board sessions. Our successful attempts to elicit large scale phenomena were of this nature, using the voice communication to ask for things to be done, but asking the poltergeist rather than Janet or Margaret, and abiding by its conditions. The validation seems to take place without needing to be imposed, in fact many obviously paranormal things do happen in these environments of their own accord. Gradually, I developed this method, in part by accident. By the time we finished there it was quite apparent that play and voice interaction could be used to generate very large scale phenomena, often seen by outside witnesses, aiming to use up energy only. This was a path that the investigators deliberately decided that they didn't want to go down, as it was creating a lot of fear in the neighbourhood. Guy apologised for taking the line he did, but my position was that he was free to do as he liked, since I was just assisting with the case.

Another example with the family present was when Guy had to leave early for some reason. This was the first time I had been left in charge for the evening. He instructed me to stay with the family in the front room and let them try to get some rest, but to sleep on the floor there that night – I had a sleeping bag and used an extra blanket below me. This worked out well and it quietened down and we all got some sleep. In the morning the family got up at their usual time 7:30 a.m. to 8:00 a.m. and I was woken by having my hair pulled rather painfully by the poltergeist. Being used to sleeping a bit later, I wanted more rest but it wouldn't let me and my hair was pulled again. Janet was in the room and could see what was happening and said I should get up. I did so and went downstairs for some toast. There weren't any more problems with phenomena that morning. It is interesting that the hair pulling seemed to be in exactly the right direction to maximise the painful sensation.

The nature of all these phenomena seems to be that it starts with some abstract system of ideas and feelings repeated internally, then internal concepts, patterns for how things should be, start being expressed without any specific knowledge or wilful direction of the manifested specific examples that fit the intent. Often there is more than one person with the same intent and this can even cause more specific detailed events to play out. This means that it is wise to exercise caution with any images that come to mind, as they can be part of the creative process and play a role in future events. The process seems to be quite general and both Hasted and myself have experienced it in other situations.

Training and learning does also seem to work. The poltergeist voice was finally happening when Janet was being watched and filmed. I operated the camera and recorded it talking despite her closed lips, tape and water in the mouth. All these controls were employed. With repetition the novelty wears off. Maurice was quite fascinated with this and we had a professional laryngograph analysis done. In my opinion the voice isn't entirely voluntary and the mechanism may not involve just the body. The sounds derive from expelled air but interacting with paranormal surfaces similar to those that Hasted found.

I brought a metal bending detector to the house. Initially this was a simple pulse counter. I would set it up and adjust it so that it wasn't sensitive to any system noise or background vibration. There was substantial paranormal activity recorded on it over quite long periods of time. We encouraged the production of the phenomena. Later, I brought a full setup with sensors embedded inside a short metal bar and chart recorder too. Once it had been set up in the bedroom, and allowed to run quietly for some time, Janet was invited to have a go. I explained that she wasn't to touch the bar but she could put her hand a few inches away at the side if she wished. After a few minutes a few small signals were visible on the chart and I encouraged her to build up the effect. When they were larger she could produce bursts on command or stop them. This is important for validation. I turned down the sensitivity of the chart recorder. As expected the signals grew larger to keep the audible pen sounds going, and finally the bar became bent without touch. The signals had an odd characteristic since, with other families, we usually found abrupt single pulses or perhaps step like bends, sometimes with exponential decay due to relaxation. In this session there were oscillatory waves at between four and eight cycles a second. Hasted commented on how unusual this was and we eventually concluded that she, or whatever agency was at work, had learned to produce oscillations as these maximised the rate at which the earlier pulse counter would be triggered. Presumably with faster changes there is some limiting effect. I tried a subsequent session with metal bending but didn't get any positive results. This does happen with metal-bending children in other families, too, at times. Maurice and Guy didn't think it worth keeping on with this line of research, but Janet did visit Birkbeck at a later time.

Play and excitement generally encourage the effects. This didn't seem to happen so much if the poltergeist voice wasn't involved, but when it was I was able to ask it to do things in front of the girls, but I was told to leave the room. We started with vanishing small objects. I would come into the room to help find them and, as this could be difficult, we soon moved onto larger things, which were more difficult to hide. We did these experiments over a few days and I asked the voice if it could lift the girls up, which it agreed to do. We started with short levitations and moved on to somersaults, the girl being lifted would scream at that point and the other describe what was happening. I also asked about taking things next door and was, in the end, able to get it to agree to lift both girls and take them there. There was screaming from them both and then an eerie silence, at which point I started to wonder if I might have gone too far. I was just thinking if I should go in when their screams restarted. What they described was going through into some sort of lit room but one without a window. That was enough for the day so we decided to stop. However, a book was later discovered next door. Guy used these events in his book describing the case. The going through the wall isn't unique: there is another case that I know of in Asia where a girl described being carried into a wall and up through the roof of the house. Also one of the metal-bending boys that Hasted knew was able to levitate in his bedroom, draw on the ceiling and take photos whilst up there, etc. He also described a box-like energy surface around him with irregularities similar to the surface of a magnetic fluid.

We elaborated these methods to use up the energy of the girls. Hasted suggested doing this so that there would be less disturbance in the evenings. It seems to be effective as long as the focus is on this and not on collecting evidence of the paranormal. That often follows later, anyway. It can end up producing some large effects and these seem to be safe and fairly well controlled. However, care has to be used as it can affect others outside the family and this can be a problem for everyone concerned. Outsiders usually have not been through the gradual familiarisation and can become frightened when seeing things for the first time. Guy and Maurice did try to involve other people in the case at times, just as Hasted would let other interested scientists sit in on his sessions with families. I have personal experience of how difficult this can be with newspaper reporters having their own agenda, which they often follow on the basis of a single session and in the face of the evidence. The poltergeist phenomenon is also somewhat more difficult to work with. It isn't possible to turn new people loose on the family unsupervised; they might see more things this way and get a better experience but it would cause harm to the household. The investigators are generally providing support and some therapy to a disturbed environment; they develop their own ways of redirecting the energy. Outsiders usually expect immediately to see paranormal events, as with those they have heard about right at the start of a case. They often don't have the patience to join the team for an extended period. Research is conducted over long periods with multiple sessions; single ones usually tell you very little. It is possible to redirect the energy into a more useful form by training and habituation but, even so, this often isn't the primary goal of many poltergeist investigators.

I was working on this case as an assistant to more experienced investigators and, fortunately, they were generally quite good at interpreting what was going on and dealing with other interested parties. Hasted helped Maurice and Guy to avoid common mistakes as he had substantial experience of working with young people and looking at what is really being asked and the responsibilities of an investigator in what subsequently happens; also how to attempt to do things and encourage this through the right environment. Later, I was asked to make a report by the SPR, something that I had no skill or experience of doing at that time. It is a common mistake to expect everyone involved in a case to be able to produce written reports. Maurice and Guy usually used tape recorders and verbal interviews. I believe that if there is felt to be a need to produce formal documentation then there should be guidelines available and someone responsible for helping to use these to write up reports as witnesses direct. Another example of this is with the report forms, which were brought to Enfield at one time. The person with the forms should, for example, have known that it was formally wrong for them to offer to fill out all the details at the top later. They should also have been more skilled at eliciting the background sequence of events and reasons behind what was happening and why people were doing what they were doing to achieve better documentation; not just being content with getting some sort of writing on a piece of paper. In my view this was the real difference with the more professional investigators. Poltergeist outbreaks are situations where there is psychological distress and I believe that Maurice and Guy both took this aspect seriously and did a lot of good in the Enfield Case.

The only other thing I might want to add at this stage is about the difficulty of those times. When Jason

[Engwer] first asked me to start remembering my experiences in the house there, it was something that I found quite uncomfortable and a bit unpleasant going into. It isn't about any of the people: I found them all very likable and easy to get on with, more so than usual. It was difficult because of the disturbance that everyone was subjected to, and the hard times; I didn't have much money to spare and the same applied to the family. There wasn't much variation in terms of trips out for the girls. As an example, the voice was trying to get me to take them out to the park in exchange for seeing levitation. We did get permission from their mum to have a short excursion, and later I discussed this with Maurice. He thought that there had to be a set limit to involvement with the family. This feeling has lessened over the last few months but still leaves me puzzled when I think about it because it is difficult to pinpoint an exact cause. I also can't think of any other times in my life that have induced such a difficult feeling as this. I suspect that it may also be the case for other people, perhaps more strongly so for them than for me.

I'll finish with one last point: it is also interesting that yogis of eastern origin often make a habit of meditating on good feelings and building these up. They do seem to relate to psychic phenomena in general, so perhaps it isn't so surprising in a poltergeist case.

Graham Morris

[Graham Morris telephoned me on 10 January 2019. An edited version of our conversation, printed below, was made immediately afterwards.] Although he did not agree with all the goings-on at Enfield he was overall still very positive about it and believed that there was a "force" that was seemingly unleashed by Janet during her pre-pubescent period. He mentioned that "books would fly around her classroom at school" and that "tins would come off the shelves in shops". He remembered that on the first night of attendance, when he was initially next door, it was when Janet came into the Hodgsons' house that everything started to happen "with a bang". His opinion was that there was "pure physics" taking place and that the phenomena would eventually be explained just like many other types of originally unknown forces had been, such as electromagnetism.

CHAPTER SIX

Discussion

The reader will have noticed my avoidance of the word 'conclusion' for this final chapter. If there is one thing I have learned during my time delving into the world of psychical research it is that as soon as one reaches a conclusion it gets overturned by new evidence coming to light, usually just after one has made one's deliberations public! There is a very good chance that no one will ever know for CERTAIN what really happened during the Enfield investigation between 1977 and 1978 and I certainly do not either! This does not stop me from expressing what I would hope to be a reasonably well-informed opinion.

Perhaps the best one can achieve is to set out the possibilities and then let the reader make his or her own mind up. I have attempted this in my previous books, some of which presented photographs of alleged ghosts or other paranormal phenomena. I published the photographs; explained what the photographers had thought they had discovered and then let the readers make their own minds up with as much knowledge about the circumstances and provenance of the shooting as possible. Graham Morris took many photographs, during his time in Enfield, which have been open to different interpretations. Playfair (2007) claimed they provided "good hard evidence" making the accounts of activity more inclined to be believed, but he also contradicted this statement by writing that photographs "... can not only lie, but also deceive us in a number of ways ..." (Willin, 2008).

Under the heading of 'Fantastical poltergeists' Gauld listed in his book (1979) six possible categories of phenomena that might be included in two specific cases that he had researched, namely the 'Sandfeldt poltergeist' of 1722 and the 'Poona poltergeist' of 1927-30. He listed these categories as:

1. Object-movements
2. Apport phenomena
3. Intelligence and responsiveness
4. Apparitions
5. Levitation and transportation of people
6. Transition to assault

In the 'Enfield Poltergeist Case' there was, of course, the further demonstration of the voice phenomena and, in the 'Mount Rainier Case', the appearance of the scratch marks on Roland's body. However, the actual source of all these occurrences needs careful thought, which Gauld and Cornell give to the matter in the second half of their book. In the introduction to this book I suggested that the reader might accept any or none of a list of possible answers to the alleged disturbances. They were "spirit entities; psychic forces; mistaken interpretations; hallucinations; naughty children or any other source". Let us give these interpretations a little more thought.

Spirit entities

I suspect that these two words are so heavily 'loaded' that there will be many different interpretations as to what they actually mean. Almost certainly I think there is an implication that we are talking about something outside of our current knowledge as science would dictate and therefore open to considerable argument. People of a religious persuasion might be happy to embrace the possibility of spirits in some form or the other and 'entities' might appeal to the many who accept visitors from different worlds from our own – possibly extra-terrestrials. Much as I might like to embrace either or both of these possibilities, currently I require more evidence, please, since my current belief system doesn't accommodate them.

Psychic forces

Once again one must ask oneself what is meant by "psychic forces". Psychical research and parapsychology have both sought and seemingly found evidence for such non-physical capabilities. Sceptics, in the wrong sense of the word, refuse to accept the possibility of extra sensory perception, psycho-kinesis and other capabilities, but one might wonder whether the same people would have refuted hypnotism and placebo effects in the past. The mind (whatever that is) does seem to be able to override the body in ways which are not necessarily brain-orientated … unless, of course, we just haven't yet found out how it works in certain ways. If this is true then surely science should continue to explore these anomalies and sceptics, in the right sense of the word, should do just that. Were psychic forces at work in Enfield? I think there is a strong possibility of this at times.

Mistaken interpretations

We often see what we either want to see or don't want to see! Examples of pareidolia and simulacra infiltrate our daily lives with or without our necessarily being conscious of them. Gauld & Cornell refer to this as "motivated seeing". If I may offer a personal – and what proved to be a humorous – example of a mistaken interpretation from my own experiences …

The date was late October 1975 and a colleague and I were visiting Bolton Abbey, North Yorkshire where "ghostly chanting" had been heard. It was daytime and I was armed with a video-recorder. The place was seemingly deserted. As we approached the door the faint sound of chanting could be heard and I turned on my machine, which registered sound input. Cautiously we opened the door to find the church empty, but the sound of the chanting was louder inside. At that point we might have fled the scene taking our PROOF with us, however, we remained steadfast. After a couple of minutes a lady appeared from the vestry; said hello to us and asked whether we minded her playing her tape of plainsong since she liked some uplifting company while she did the cleaning! One wonders how many times mistaken interpretations occurred at Enfield? Objects can topple over seemingly of their own accord when a vibration or a knock has happened and the human memory as to where things have been placed is particularly fallible. Machinery does break down for no apparent reason, particularly after changes of temperature or after being jolted during a journey. However, equally there are cases of equipment malfunction, which are not generally identifiable. For instance, during an exorcism at a property in Cornwall:

> Oddly enough the householder's daughter was using a video recorder during the clergyman's requiem for the dead woman, and it was found that at the time he was conducting his blessing, the tape wiped itself clean – and that the magnetic structure of the tape had been so changed that it was no longer possible to record on the tape. Subsequently this tape was checked by an engineer, who was totally unable to explain what had happened to it. (Underwood, 1990, p. 43)

Hallucinations

The idea of hallucination cannot be encompassed when hard objects were discovered after allegedly being thrown through the air. However, there were several examples of apparitions being encountered in the Hodgsons' house, which raises the question of their origin. The human eyesight is not good at viewing fleeting glimpses in peripheral vision, which can lead to either mistaken interpretations again or possible hallucinations. Although of no particular relevance to the 'Enfield Poltergeist Case', hypnagogic and hypnopompic sleep are often cited, rightly or wrongly, for ghostly visions at the start or end of sleep. The states of the percipient's mind or general health – notably eyesight – will also have a bearing on such sightings. Vic Tandy's work even suggested that infrasound might cause visual hallucinations (See Parsons, 2012). Whether the partial and full apparitions that were witnessed in the Hodgsons' house were genuine or otherwise will probably never be known and the veracity of the sightings must, therefore, remain with the reader's opinion.

Naughty children

… or what more harshly might be referred to as FRAUD! Fraud was detected in forty-one of the five hundred cases (8%) that Gauld & Cornell researched in their magnum opus *Poltergeists* (1979) and certainly there were also examples of this at Enfield. It was admitted to at times and certainly accepted by Grosse and Playfair as happening. The questions needing answers are, were *all* the incidents caused by childish pranks and the like and, if not, then how many times did the children hoodwink the investigators? I contacted the psychologist Chris French since he had made various negative comments about the case (2016). He provided clarifications about his comments referring to various aspects of the case. Concerning the alleged levitations he stated, "Of course, if it was genuine levitation it might look the same – but Occam's Razor would favour the hoax hypothesis. The latter is not proven, just, in my opinion, a lot more likely" (Private correspondence). He felt that it was perfectly plausible that the reliability of the eyewitnesses was "very unreliable" and that the case did not fit into the possibility of being "a proven white crow". Grosse stated on 9 November 1977 that he believed that "95% was genuine" and, in December 1978, Playfair spoke about "thirty incidents" that he believed to be genuine. It must have been very difficult to observe, at times, four children who all had tendencies to misbehave, especially when, frustratingly, so much of the alleged phenomena occurred behind closed doors or generally out of sight. I do not want to give a percentage to faked or genuine phenomena, other than to comment that, from having heard the evidence of the tapes, I would not agree with Grosse that 95% would have been genuine.

Any other sources

Dear reader, this is where you may wish to have an input into subsequent editions of this book! If you believe that you have appropriate ideas that have not been covered by the above, then send them in to me via the publisher and we shall see whether we can include them.

It seems far-fetched to me to believe that there was just one answer to the Enfield poltergeist manifestations. In reality all, or at least some, of the above categories might have been apparent in different situations. However, I maintain, what is of paramount importance is the possibility that just one single incident may have had a paranormal origin whereupon the current scientific paradigm needs to be adjusted. One white crow if you wish!

APPENDICES

APPENDIX 1

Who's Who

There has been considerable confusion in some publications concerning the names of the people involved with the 'Enfield Poltergeist Case' through the use of pseudonyms, notably by Guy Playfair. This was understandable at the time to protect the identities of the people concerned. However, their names have appeared in the public domain for many years now and I do not feel the need to continue to use pseudonyms. I shall not use any people's current surnames if they have changed their names through marriage etc. and will accordingly identify them by the name they were using and mainly called at the time of the investigation. I have also mentioned, briefly, their role in the case. Use of 'Reporter' means they either submitted a report concerning their visit/s or were involved with the case in a more than perfunctory way. It does not mean they were necessarily a journalist-style reporter. Some 'Visitors' witnessed phenomena, but not necessarily to any great extent.

Alan, Ray	Ventriloquist. Visitor.
Annett, David	Pye product manager. Visitor.
Bannister, Paul	Journalist. Visitor.
Barrington, Mary Rose	Lawyer/ psychical researcher. Reporter
Beloff, John	Psychologist. Visitor.
Bence, Douglas	Journalist. Visitor.
Bender, Hans	Parapsychologist. Adviser.
Bentley, Neil	Journalist. Visitor.
Berger, Lawrence	Dental surgeon. Secondary investigator.
Besant, Maisie	Medium. Visitor.
Burcombe, Denise	Witness to some of the phenomena.
Burcombe, John	Hospital Deputy Head Porter. Primary witness to the phenomena.
Burcombe, Paul	Witness to some of the phenomena.
Burcombe, Sylvie	Witness to some of the phenomena.
Carr, Bernard	Astronomer/Psychical researcher. Reporter.
Christopher, Milbourne	Magician. Visitor.

Cornell, Tony	Psychical researcher. Reporter.
Davis, Clifford	TV critic. Visitor.
Dear, Peter	Visitor.
Denney, R. H.	Pye chief demonstrator. Visitor.
Fallows, George	Journalist. Visitor.
Fenwick, Peter	Neuropsychiatrist.
Fletcher, Ian	Hypnotist. Visitor.
Fuller, Elizabeth	Visitor.
Fuller, John	Author. Reporter.
Gasparetto, Elsie	Psychic. Visitor.
Gasparetto, Luiz	Psychic. Visitor.
Gauld, Alan	Psychologist/ Psychical researcher. Reporter.
Gladden, Rose	Healer. Advisor.
Gmelig-Meyling, Dono	Medium. Visitor.
Grattan-Guinness, Ivor	Historian. Visitor.
Grattan-Guinness, Mrs.	Visitor.
Gregory, Anita	Psychical researcher. Reporter.
Grosse, Betty	Visitor
Grosse, Marilyn	Scientist. Visitor.
Grosse, Maurice	Inventor. Joint main investigator.
Grosse, Richard	Solicitor. Reporter.
Hallson, Peter	Psychical researcher. Reporter.
Hasted, John	Physicist. Visitor.
Hearn, Ronald	Medium. Advisor.

Heeps, Carolyn	Policewoman. Reporter.
Hitch, Don	Sound recording engineer. Visitor.
Hodgson, Billy	Partial focus of activity.
Hodgson, Janet	Main focus of activity.
Hodgson, Johnny	Witness.
Hodgson, Margaret	Secondary focus.
Hodgson, Mr.	Possible witness to some phenomena.
Hodgson, Mrs.	Primary witness to much of the phenomena.
Huxley, Francis	Anthropologist. Visitor.
Kennedy, Charles	Bill Wilkins' friend.
Liefhebber, Peter	Dutch journalist. Visitor.
Manning, Matthew	Psychic healer. Visitor.
Martin, David	TV producer, Visitor.
Miura, Professor	Japanese academic [?]. Visitor.
Morris, Graham	Photographer. Reporter.
Morris, Rosalind	Producer. Visitor.
Moses, Charles	Psychical researcher, Reporter.
Nottingham, Gary	Visitor.
Nottingham, Peggy	Witness to phenomena.
Nottingham, Vic.	Witness to phenomena.
O'Keeffe, Eleanor	Secretary. Reporter.
Pearce, Daphne	Speech-therapist, Visitor.

Pearce-Higgins, Canon	Vice Provost, Southwark Cathedral. Advisor.
Pincott, Hugh	Psychical researcher. Reporter.
Playfair, Guy Lyon	Author/ Psychical researcher. Joint main investigator.
Playfair, J. H. L.	Immunologist. Visitor.
Rainbow, John	Tradesman, Witness.
Richardson, Mr.	Peggy Nottingham's father. Visitor.
Rimmer, Bryan	Journalist. Visitor.
Robertson, David	Physicist. Reporter.
Roy, Archie	Astronomer, President Scottish SPR. Advisor.
Sargent, Carl	Parapsychologist. Reporter.
Scott, Mr	Policeman. Visitor.
Sherrick, Gerry	Medium/ taxi driver. Visitor.
Short, Hazel	Crossing patrol operative. Witness.
Stiles, John	Psychical researcher. Reporter.
Stone, Peter	Photographer. Visitor.
Sutton, Gloria	Gary Nottingham's girlfriend. Witness.
Thorpe, David	Photographer. Visitor.
Twigg, Ena	Medium. Advisor.

"Voices":

Andrew Garner
Barney
Bill Wilkins
Cacheerio Ash
Charlie
Claude
Dirty Dick
Fred
George Mace
Hondy Garner
Joe
Ralph
Stewart Carrick
Stewart Surtan
Tommy
Zebedee

Warren, Ed & Lorraine — Paranormal investigators/demonologists. Visitors.

Wilkins, Terry — Bill Wilkins' son.

APPENDIX 2

The Alleged Phenomena

The paranormal phenomena that occurred in Enfield are extensive and varied. A tentative list would include all that is listed below and probably other examples that have either escaped the microphone or my probing ears.

Apparitions
Ashtray   thrown

Bed   impression on
                                - thrown out of
                                - dragged under
                                - turned over
                                - shaking
Bedclothes   shaking
                                - moving
Books   moving
Bottle/s   jumping
Boxes   thrown
Brushes   jumping

Carpet   movement
Chairs   movement
Clock   jumping
Clothing   movement
Coins   appearing
                                - dropping
Cold breezes
Crockery   movement
Cupboard   jumping
Curtain   movement
Curtain "attacks" Janet
Cushion   jumps
Cutlery   jumps

Door   opens by itself
Door chimes   swinging
Drawers   falling
                                - opening

Electrical	malfunctions
Excrement	smeared
Fires	
Fish tank lid flies off table	
Flower pot	movement
Footsteps	unknown source
Furniture	movement
Ice cubes	appear
Iron	levitates
Iron grill from fireplace thrown	
Items (various) piled up	
Kicked	
Kitchen (various) activity	
Knockings (rappings, tapping etc.)	
Lamp	movement
Leads	pulled from socket
Lego bricks	flying
Levitation	Janet
Light phenomena	
Marbles	flying
Mug	jumps
Mug of water appears	
Notebook	jumps
Paper tissues appear	
Paper tissue lands on Grosse's head	
People	pulled/pushed
Physical assault	

Picture pulled off wall	
Pillow	flying
Plastic rod	materializes
Poster	movement
Refrigerator	moved
Saucepan	takes off
Slippers	thrown
Smells	
Sofa (settee) jumps/ turns over	
Spoon/ metal bending	
Stones	thrown
Table	turns over
Teapot	movement
Tin	jumps
Toilet	self-flushes
Whistling	
Xmas decorations ripped down	
Xmas tree	jumps

APPENDIX 3

Dates

The precise dates of the combined recordings which are held in the audio-visual archives of the Society for Psychical Research are as follows:

September 1977
10, 11, 19, 21, 28, 29, 30.
October 1977
2, 3, 4, 5, 6, 10, 11, 12, 14, 15, 16, 17, 19, 20, 22, 23, 24, 25, 26, 27, 28.
November 1977
5, 6, 7, 8, 9, 10, 11, 12, 13, 14, 15, 23, 26, 27, 28, 29, 30.
December 1977
1, 2, 3, 4, 5, 7, 8, 10, 11, 12, 13, 14, 15, 16, 17, 18, 19, 21, 22, 23, 27, 28, 30.
January 1978
1, 2, 3, 4, 5, 6, 8, 9, 10, 13, 14, 16, 18, 19, 20, 21, 22, 23, 24, 26, 27, 28, 29, 30.

February 1978

1, 2, 4, 6, 8, 9, 10, 11, 13, 16, 17, 18, 19, 22, 24, 25, 26.

March 1978

1, 11, 14, 19, 20, 29.

April 1978

5, 9, 10, 13, 16, 19, 23, 24, 27.

May 1978

1, 8, 11, 15, 18, 30, 31

June 1978

1, 4, 7, 8, 12, 15, 16, 19, 29 and unspecified.

July 1978

10, 13, 27, 28.

August 1978

21, 24.

September 1978

11, 14.

October 1978

2, 6.

April 1979

3, 8, 20, 21, 23, 25.

May 1979

10, 20.

August 1979

14.

October 1981

12

SUGGESTED
READING/LISTENING

Allen, Thomas (1994). *Possessed*. London: Corgi. ISBN 0-552-14144-5.

Andreas, Peter (1978). 'Der Poltergeist von Enfield'. *Esotera*. July 598-603.

Bannister, Paul (1978). 'Supernatural being speaks through three children in terrorized family'. *National Enquirer*. 18 June.

Barbanell, Maurice (1977). 'Poltergeist Makes Page 1'. *Psychic News*. 17 September.

Barrington, Mary Rose (1983). 'Correspondence'. *Journal of the Society for Psychical Research*, Vol. 52, no. 794. 155-156.

Berger, Lawrence (1980). 'Correspondence'. *Journal of the Society for Psychical Research*, Vol. 50, no. 784. 420-421.

Blatty, William Peter (1998). *Before the Exorcist*. Eye, Suffolk: ScreenPress Books.

Brinkley, Bill (1949). 'Pastor tells eerie tale of 'Haunted Boy''. *The Washington Post*. 10 August.

Buckland, Danny (2018). 'What I went through was real'. 'What really happened with the Enfield Poltergeist'. *Express*. 8 April.

Carlson, H. G. (1994). *Mysteries of the Unexplained*. Contemporary Books. ISBN 978-0809234974.

Clarkson, Michael (2006). *Poltergeists: Examining Mysteries of the Paranormal*. N. America: Firefly Books. ISBN 978-1554071593.

Colvin, Barrie (2010). 'The acoustic properties of unexplained rapping sounds'. *Journal of the Society for Psychical Research*. 74. 2. 65-93.

Cooke, John (1977). 'Violent ghost terrifies family and baffles police'. *The National Enquirer*.

Crabbe, John (1995). 'Maurice Grosse's tape-recorder 'Haunting''. *Psi Researcher*, no. 19. 23.

Craig, Robert (1987). 'House of Horror'. *Celebrity*. 26 November – 2 December.

Engwer, Jason (2017). 'Anita Gregory's Skepticism'. triablogue.blogspot.com/2017/05/the-enfield-poltergeist-anita-gregorys.html, Posted 8 May 2017.

Engwer, Jason (2018). 'David Robertson on the Enfield Poltergeist'.

triablogue.blogspot.com/2018/05/david-robertson-on-enfield-poltergeist.html
Posted 30 May 2018.

Erdmann, Steve (1975). 'The Truth Behind the Exorcist'. *Fate* magazine. *Info@fatemag.com.*

Fallows, George & Bence, Douglas (1977). 'The house of strange happenings'. *Daily Mirror.* 10 September.

Fodor, Nandor (1959). *On the trail of the poltergeist.* London: Arco.

Fontana, David (1991). 'A Responsive Poltergeist: A Case from South Wales'. *Journal of the Society for Psychical Research*, Vol. 57, no. 823. 385-402.

French, Chris (2002). 'Letters'. *Paranormal Review.* 22. 30.

French, Chris (2016). 'Five reasons why London's most famous poltergeist case is a hoax'. *TimeOutFilm.* 17 June.

Freud, S. and Breuer, J. (2004). *Studies in Hysteria.* London: Penguin Modern Classics.

Gauld, Alan & Cornell, A. D. (1979). *Poltergeists.* London: Routledge & Kegan Paul Ltd.

Gmelig-Meyling, Dono (1978). De boodschap van een klopgeest'. *Extra.* 1 December.

Grant, Richard (1978). 'Haunted families – are they cursed by the ghost of marital failure?" *The Daily Express.* 31 March.

Gregory, Anita (1980). 'Book Review'. *Journal of the Society for Psychical Research*, Vol. 50, no. 786. 538-431.

Gregory, Anita (1981). 'Correspondence'. *Journal of the Society for Psychical Research*, Vol. 51, no. 788. 115-116.

Gregory, Anita (1983). 'Correspondence'. *Journal of the Society for Psychical Research*, Vol. 52, no. 793. 93-95.

Gregory, Anita (1983). 'Correspondence'. *Journal of the Society for Psychical Research*, Vol. 52, no. 794. 156.

Gregory, Anita (1983). 'Problems in investigating psychokinesis in special subjects'. PhD thesis. London Metropolitan University.

Grosse, Maurice (1979). 'Correspondence'. *Journal of the Society for Psychical Research*, Vol. 50, no. 782. 258

Grosse, Maurice (1980). 'The Enfield Poltergeist'. *Alpha Magazine.* October.

Grosse, M. & Playfair, G. L. (1981). 'Correspondence'. *Journal of the Society for Psychical Research*, Vol. 51, no. 787. 34-35.

Grosse, Maurice (1981). 'Correspondence'. *Journal of the Society for Psychical Research*, Vol. 51, no. 789. 195.

Grosse, Maurice (1983). 'Correspondence'. *Journal of the Society for Psychical Research*, Vol. 52, no. 793. 92-93.

Grosse, Maurice (1994). 'Assessing the evidence'. *Psi Researcher*, no. 15. 19.

Grosse, Maurice (1994). 'Scepticism'. *Psi Researcher*, no. 12. 26.

Grosse, Maurice (1995). 'Mr Grosse replies'. *Psi Researcher*, no. 19. 23-34.

Grosse, Maurice (1997). 'Correspondence'. *Journal of the Society for Psychical Research*, Vol. 61, no. 847. 410.

Grosse, Maurice (1998). 'Correspondence'. *Journal of the Society for Psychical Research*, Vol. 63, no. 853. 61.

Grosse, Maurice (2000). 'Correspondence'. *Journal of the Society for Psychical Research*, Vol. 64. 3, no. 860. 192.

Grosse, Maurice. (2002). 'Letters'. *Paranormal Review*. 24. 27-28.

Guiley, Rosemary Ellen (1994). *The Guinness Encyclopedia of Ghosts and Spirits*. Middlesex: Guinness Publishing Ltd.

Harris, Melvin (1980). 'Correspondence'. *Journal of the Society for Psychical Research*, Vol. 50, no. 786. 552-554.

Hawkes, Rebecca (2015). 'What did the Enfield Haunting have to do with Ed and Lorraine Warren?' *The Daily Telegraph*. 12 May.

Hennessy, Val (1980). 'Phantom Fred is a force to fear'. *Evening News*. 11 June.

Houran, James (1999). 'Correspondence'. *Journal of the Society for Psychical Research*, Vol. 63, no. 856. 242-243.

Howie, Michael (2011). 'Enfield poltergeist to haunt Hollywood'. *Evening Standard*. 25 October.

Hutchinson, Mike (1998). 'Correspondence'. *Journal of the Society for Psychical Research*, Vol. 62, no. 851. 377-379.

Hyde, Deborah (2015). 'The Enfield 'Poltergeist': A Sceptic Speaks'. *The Guardian*. 1 May.

Jaffa, Sharon (2002). 'So Haunt Me'. *London Jewish News*. 26 July.

Lang, Andrew (1900). *The Making of Religion*. London: Longmans, Green. p. 129.

Liefhebber, Peter (1978). 'Mensen enmeubelen vliegen door de kamer'. *Extra*. 24 November.

Matthews, Rupert (2009). *Poltergeists and other Hauntings*. London: Arcturus Publishing Limited

Morris, Rosalind (1977). *The World This Weekend*. BBC Radio 4. 11 September.

Morris, Rosalind (1979). 'The Enfield Poltergeist'. BBC Radio 4. 26 December & 8 February.

Morris, Rosalind (1979). 'The ghost of children present'. *Evening News*. 7 February.

Moses, Charles (1979). 'The Enfield Case'. *Theta*. Vol. 7, no. 1. 1-4.

Murdie, Alan (2011). 'Look seriously at the Enfield poltergeist'. *Evening Standard* 26 October.

Myers, F. W. H. (1903). *Human Personality and its Survival of Bodily Death*. Vol. II. London: Longman, Green and Co.

Nickell, Joe (2012). 'Enfield Poltergeist Investigative Files'. *The Skeptical Inquirer* Vol. 36. 4 July/August.

Night Line. LBC Radio. 10 September 1977.

Oakes, Deborah (1989). 'Correspondence'. *Journal of the Society for Psychical Research*, Vol. 55, no. 815. 375.

Oesterreich, T. K. (1966). *Possession – Demoniacal and Other*. New Hyde Park, University Books.

Oldham, B. R. (1982). 'Correspondence'. *Journal of the Society for Psychical Research*, Vol. 51, no. 791. 321-322.

Opsasnick, Mark (1999/ 2000). *Strange Magazine*. Issue 20. Edited Mark Chorvinsky. Strangemag.com.

Opsasnick, Mark (2006) *The Real Story Behind the Exorcist: A Study of the Haunted Boy and Other True-Life Horror Legends from Around the Nation's Capital*. Xlibris.

Owen, A. R. G. (1964). *Can we explain the poltergeist?* Helix Press: New York.

Owen, A. R. G. 'Poltergeists'. *Man, Myth and Magic.* Vol. V. p. 2225.

Parsons, Steve (2012). 'Infrasound and the Paranormal'. *Journal of the Society for Psychical Research*, Vol. 76.3, no. 908. 150-174.

Penman, Danny (2007). 'Suburban poltergeist: A 30-year silence is broken'. London: *Daily Mail.* 5 March.

Petrie, Ellen (1980). 'The World Beyond'. *Daily Star.* 10 March.

Phillips, Pearson (1977). 'Knock, knock and a poltergeist calls'. *The Observer.* 6 November.

Playfair, Guy Lyon (1979). 'Poltergeist on a rampage'. *Fate.* June. 74-81.

Playfair, Guy Lyon (1980). *This House is Haunted.* Souvenir Press. Reprinted (2011) Guildford: White Crow Books. ISBN 978 1907661785.

Playfair, G. L. & Grosse, M. (1988). 'Enfield revisited – The evaporation of positive evidence'. *Journal of the Society for Psychical Research*, Vol. 55, no. 813. 208-219.

Playfair, Guy Lyon (1995). 'Enfield Effect'. *Psi Researcher.* no. 18. 23-24.

Playfair, Guy Lyon (1998). 'Correspondence'. *Journal of the Society for Psychical Research*, Vol. 62, no. 852. 475.

Playfair, G. L. & Grosse, M. (1999). 'Correspondence'. *Journal of the Society for Psychical Research*, Vol. 63, no. 857. 320-321.

Playfair, Guy Lyon (2001). 'Mediawatch'. *Paranormal Review*, 20. 14.

Price, Harry (1945). *Poltergeist*. Country Life. Reprinted (1993) London: Bracken Books.

Psychic News (1978). 'Boffins baffled by poltergeist'. 8 April.

Psychic News (1979). 'Experts testify to 'impossible' poltergeist phenomena'. 6 January.

Rankine, William (1978). 'Ghost hunters clash over mystery of spook or spoof kids'. *News of the World.* 2 April.

'Reunion. The Enfield Poltergeist'. BBC Radio 4. 8 April 2018.

Reynolds, Gillian (1978). 'Things that go bump in the night'. *The Daily Telegraph.* 27 December.

Rimmer, Bryan (1978). 'Ghost Story'. *Daily Mirror.* 30 March.

Roll, W. G. (1976). *The Poltergeist.* London: Star Books.

Scott Rogo, D. (1979). *The Poltergeist Experience.* Baltimore: Penguin Books.

Society for Psychical Research (1978). *Report of the Enfield Poltergeist Investigation Committee (EPIC).* London.

Storr, Will (2006). *Will Storr vs. The Supernatural.* London: Ebury Press.

Sutcliffe, Thomas (2007), 'It's not an apparition – this is real rubbish'. *The Independent.* 7 March

Thurston, Herbert S. J. (1953). *Ghosts and Poltergeists.* London: Burns Oates.

Underwood, Peter (1990). *Exorcism*. London: Robert Hale.

(The) Unexplained (1980 onwards). Multiple articles. London: Orbis Publishing Ltd.

Willin, Melvyn (2007). 'Haunted House'. *The Independent*. 15 March.

Willin, Melvyn (2008). *The Paranormal Caught on Film*. Newton Abbot: David & Charles.

Willin, Melvyn (2015). 'The Enfield Poltergeist'. *Psi Encyclopedia.*

https://psi-encyclopedia.spr.ac.uk/articles/enfield-poltergeist

Woodforde, John (1979). 'Alarming girls'. *The Sunday Telegraph*. 11 February.

Wright, Terry (1994). *The Sceptical Occultist*. London: Random House.

www.enfieldhaunting.co.uk/

INDEX OF NAMES

Lightning Source UK Ltd.
Milton Keynes UK
UKHW010624040320
359751UK00001B/103